ON THE THIRD DAY

Re-looking at the Resurrection

JOHN QUERIPEL

WIPF & STOCK · Eugene, Oregon

Wipf and Stock Publishers
199 W 8th Ave, Suite 3
Eugene, OR 97401

On the Third Day
Re-Looking at the Resurrection
By Queripel, John
Copyright © 2018 by Queripel, John All rights reserved.
Softcover ISBN-13: 979-8-3852-6604-3
Hardcover ISBN-13: 979-8-3852-6605-0
eBook ISBN-13: 979-8-3852-6606-7
Publication date 10/13/2025
Previously published by Morning Star Publishing, 2018

This edition is a scanned facsimile of the original edition published in 2018.

Contents

Preface 5

Chapter One 11
    Dying and rising gods of antiquity

Chapter Two 17
    Sheol's shadow to dry bones rising

Chapter Three 27
    The grave transcended

Chapter Four 31
    Jesus' understanding and practice

Chapter Five 57
    Jesus' Resurrection - Gospel truth?

Chapter Six 105
    The deeper evidence

Postlude 129

Preface

Voices ranging from tub thumping fundamentalists to reasonable sounding evangelicals speak today of the need for Christians to believe in the literal bodily resurrection of Jesus. Yet, quite clearly the scientific modern understanding of a post-Enlightenment world makes it increasingly difficult for growing numbers of people, including believers, to believe in that form of the resurrection, which would have the actual en-fleshed corporeal body of Jesus walking from the tomb and being present again upon the earth. For many this seems to be a crude, even vulgar, image which just will not wash in the modern world. Are there then alternatives to this view, or is it necessary to do away with the idea of resurrection per-se and if we do away with the resurrection, can Christianity then survive?

I want to suggest that indeed there are alternatives, and that the commonly held view of a physical resurrection, whereby Jesus in en-fleshed form walked from the cave of his entombment, miraculously rolling the stone away, being resurrected to the earth whereupon he remained in physical form for some 40 days, before ascending to the heavens, and only then existing in another form beyond the physical, represents a very late development in the Scriptural tradition. This late developing tradition, with a time-line built primarily around the Lukan story, became, however, the orthodox view, the one taught in the catechism, and the one in which if you didn't literally believe, you were in past times in danger of being tossed to the fire, and here I don't mean those of hell, but rather the very more prosaic fires prepared by the church and civic authorities. Yet this still orthodox view of the resurrection, and therefore the one held by most Christians, but rejected by an increasing number of others, as being the only permissible view of the resurrection, is preceded by an earlier tradition, a tradition not from outside, but rather from within the Christian Scriptural tradition at its earliest level, at least 30-50 years earlier than that which became the basis for Christian orthodoxy.

In our exploration we shall find that the earliest Christian tradition had Jesus resurrected, not in physical form, and not to the earth, but instead directly to the heavens. That resurrection was experienced not as physical contact nor proven by physical evidences such as the consumption of food, touch, stones miraculously rolled away, or by grave-clothes so left they allow those who first sight them to know that resurrection had taken place, but rather in the far more subjective realm of appearances or epiphanies. This is the resurrection spoken by Paul, writing in the fifties and early sixties of the first century, only some 20-30 years after the event being described.

The Christian faith presupposes the resurrection of Jesus Christ as being its central tenet and without it, it is claimed there can be no Christian faith. Such a claim was made from very early days in the faith. The apostle Paul claims, 'If Christ has not been raised, your faith is futile,' (1 Cor 15:17) while the earliest Christian preaching references it. (Acts 1:22, 2:24- 33, 3:14-21, 4;10, 33, 10:40-41 13:30-31, 1 Cor 15, Phil 3:10, Eph 1:19-23, Col 2:12-13, Rom 6:5, 1 Pet 1:3, 3:21) Indeed, the resurrection is present in every book of the Christian Scriptures, while interpreting the texts in a manner not possible for us, the writers of the Christian Scriptures saw the resurrection as being foretold in numerous texts of the Hebrew Scriptures. (Acts 2:25-36, 1 Cor 15:4) [1]

Clearly, belief in the resurrection is very early and widespread in the Christian tradition. The first biographical account we have of it comes in the Book of Acts, where we are thrice told of Paul being struck down by the vision of the risen Christ on the road to Damascus. (Acts 9:1-19, 22:6-16, 26:12-16) This account makes clear that the community present in that city, as represented by Ananias, already believed in the resurrection. (Acts 9:10-18) Given that Paul's conversion experience occurs early in the 6th decade of the first century, it is evident that in just some 20 years Christian belief in the resurrection had been sufficiently established to lead to a Christian community in Damascus founded on that belief.

For reason of the resurrection's central part in the earliest testimony even moderate and progressive Christians, while they may be prepared to give up other inexplicable miracles of the faith such as the virgin birth, incarnation and the miracles, refuse to give up the resurrection. There is something about

---

[1] It has become customary now to call what Christians have called the Old Testament, the Hebrew or Jewish Scriptures, and that which Christians have called the New Testament, the Christian or Greek Scriptures. Obviously the term New suggests that the Old is superseded and it is for this reason, the avoidance of what is called supercessionalism, that this parlance has become more widely used.

the resurrection without which, as Paul has claimed, the faith makes no sense. If it cannot be saved can the Christian faith itself be saved?

It was that profound belief in the resurrection of Jesus among those who had followed him during his lifetime, and then deserted him at the time of his crucifixion, which was the seed of the movement that would eventually become known as Christianity. The deep impact this belief had on those who believed can be easily seen in a number of ways. The first is in the great change undergone by those who had deserted Jesus at the time of his trial and crucifixion. They soon after that desertion turned from fear and cowardice to being daring witnesses, (see for example Acts 4:5-22) so brave that eventually, according to the tradition, all except one of the original close circle would be martyred for this belief.[2] That transformative power of the resurrection belief can also be seen in a few other ways, each of which depends on our remembering that all of the very earliest followers of Jesus were Jewish. In light of the ultimate Gentile nature of the church we can very easily forget this. These earliest Jewish followers of Jesus kept the wider Jewish traditions, these maintained by some right up unto the fifth century, when Chrysostom in a homily full of anti-Semitic vitriol felt a need to tell Christians to cease attending synagogue.[3] I have seen it best to call these earliest believers, initially all Jews, 'Jesus Jews', a term picking up both their being Jews, and also their following of this Jesus, who of course himself lived and died in the Jewish context and tradition. Yet, this profound resurrection experience changed those early Jewish followers in a couple of ways, evidencing clearly both its power and reality for them.

The first of these is that community's view of Jesus. Though shaped by a strict Jewish orthodoxy regarding the transcendence and oneness of God, they would quickly embark on a path where Jesus would become progressively elevated in importance, to a point within the later layers of the Christian Scriptures he would even be regarded as divine. Just some thirty years after his death, Paul, a good orthodox Jew could exclaim, 'that

---

[2] I use the term 'close circle' her than the twelve for 'the twelve' is clearly a number which is artificial. It reflects the Church's desire to be understood as a new Israel under twelve new patriarchs, part of the reason as to why also they are all male. Even to count those named in the gospels is to arrive at more than twelve.
[3] John Chrysostom, Against the Jews. Homily 1

at the name of Jesus every knee shall bow, in heaven, on earth, and in the depths; and every tongue confess, Jesus Christ is Lord.' (Phil 2:10-11) This is truly a remarkable statement for one so strongly schooled in a tradition that would have vowed such as anathema. This statement comes as the conclusion of a passage in which he claims that, 'Christ Jesus, who though he was in the form of God, did not count equality with God, a thing to be grasped, but emptied himself taking the form of a servant, being born in human form.' (Phil 2:6-7) Quite clearly here Paul understands Jesus as being ontologically distinct from ordinary human beings, for why else this kenotic (self-emptying) description of Jesus in order to become human? What is even more amazing is that this passage from Paul, as early as it is, appears to be a liturgical piece (a hymn, litany or creed) which goes back even earlier. That further elevation of Jesus would continue until at the Council of Nicea in 325 CE,[4] by which time he had reached the status of being of the same substance as God the Father, and co-eternal with him.[5]

The second of these profound changes regards the Shabbat or Sabbath. Sabbath observance was deeply sacred to the Jewish community, and yet within one generation these Jesus Jews, while continuing to attend Sabbath worship at the synagogue began to see Sunday as their prime day of worship. It has been said in jest, it is almost impossible to get a congregation to change their time of worship by one hour, so to get a change to a whole new day must mean something momentous happened! What was it that caused these Jewish believers, who continued to observe the Shabbat to also feel that they needed to worship this one on the day

---

[4] The accepted way of dating today has increasingly become C.E. (the Common Era) and B.C.E. (Before the Common Era), the supposed dating of Jesus' birth being still, however, the dividing line.

[5] The question of the status of Jesus as understood by the writers of the Christian Scriptural is well fought over. Clearly they view him as the Messiah but within Judaism it was not expected that the Messiah would be divine so saying Jesus is Messiah does not make him divine. Clearly the status of Jesus for the early Christians, nearly all of them Jewish, was immensely high. Nowhere in the Jewish Scriptures do we find Moses, Elijah or David having such status imputed to them as does Jesus among his followers. Larry W. Hurtado argues cogently that this elevation of Jesus to such high status begins very early and does so rising to divinity strictly from within a Jewish context before there is any association of Jesus with the pagan dying and rising god. That such happens within a strictly monotheistic tradition speaks of the astonishing impact Jesus made on his followers. Larry W. Hurtado, William B Eerdmans Publishing Co, United States, 2006

following, Sunday being chosen as it was the day on which it was believed that he rose?

Obviously something highly dramatic must have happened to cause these great changes. People after-all don't suddenly become heroic in the face of the same danger which had caused the demise of their leader without reason. What happened to transform these people, 'behind locked doors,' (John 20:19) into being fearless witnesses for Christ? It has been said that that their distress was such that they experienced a wish fulfillment, that Jesus, the one in whom they had placed such hope was not dead, but rather had been miraculously raised, not on the last day, which orthodoxy at that time suggested he would, but rather presently in their own time and context. This however is to suggest such an investiture by all of his closest circle and a number of others, that they each suffered some type of self-projected illusion, a mass psychosis. That, I would suggest is highly unlikely. If one of 'the twelve,' Judas, had seemingly first become embittered because of dashed hopes of Jesus operating as the expected Messiah of power, thereby taking the action he did, it is likely that a number of the others, likewise embittered at Jesus' failure, would, have like Judas, turned against the movement, or at least would have returned to the quiet safe ordinary life of their trades, mainly fishing. Indeed, the Scriptures tell us that this is precisely what did happen, before that transformational experience called resurrection changed them forever. (John 21:2-3) Given t there were many more followers of Jesus than 'the twelve,' are we to suspect all shared in this mass psychosis? The resurrection experience, I believe, is far more complex than such.

Likewise, people don't lightly make a change to something so deeply acculturated, universally held in a deeply religious society, as their day of worship. For Jews, both at the time of Jesus, and now, the Shabbat is viewed as one of the most important distinguishing things in their faith. That these 'Jesus Jews' added to their Sabbath worship another celebration held on the day of resurrection – Sunday, as said – again suggests that something highly significant occurred on that Sunday we have come to know as Easter Day.

Further, as already noted, what event could have been so significant for those following Jesus, all of them good monotheist Jews, to so rapidly hold Jesus in such high status so, that absolutely contrary to that most deep seated in their faith tradition – absolute monotheism – they would very early begin to elevate him on the path to divinity?

All of these things can only point to something incredibly dramatic happening, which both they and we can call resurrection. We cannot, I assert, get at the actuality of the event, but only at its effects. It is those effects, however, which represent its strongest evidence. From the effects we can work backward to hypothesise about the actual event, clearly inaccessible in itself. From these effects we may even create scenarios or stories about the actual event and that, I charge, is precisely what the gospel writers did. The fantastic stories of a physically raised Jesus suddenly appearing in closed rooms, displaying his wounds to Thomas, admonishing Mary in the garden not to touch him, of stones being rolled away, and grave-clothes miraculously evidencing the reality of the resurrection are precisely that – stories created to get some type of grasp on that which in reality is beyond human grasping.

The physicality of the resurrection stories has also another purpose, as a means of countering Gnostic forms of faith which threatened to subsume the Christian gospel. At the heart of Gnosticism was an anti-material view which radically deprecated anything to do with the flesh. Such a religious outlook represented a very real threat to a faith, that at its core had an appreciation of the material. Such appreciation is clearly seen in God having created the material world, liberated people from the very physical bondage of slavery in Egypt, proclaimed the Law or Torah, which contrary to nearly all religious codes at that time, spoke strongly of material concerns in living together, the revelation given through the prophets and their calling for just human relationships, and last of all becoming incarnate, en-fleshed as Jesus Christ, within the material world.

Essentially, I argue resurrection is a deep experience, transformative in its power, with it being in that dimension we find its greatest 'proof.' That we as human beings find it hard to live with such un-objectified mysteries is what gives rise to the stories, these also having a theological purpose, refutation of Gnostic anti-material spiritualism.

Of course in antiquity Jesus wasn't the only one present upon the earth held to be divine who had died and risen and it is with this subject we commence.

Chapter One

Dying and rising gods of antiquity

In antiquity Jesus was not the only dying and rising god; far from it, as even a cursory study of that epoch will show. The pagan religious milieu is full of such stories, the dying and rising often taking place over three days.

The concept of a dying-and-rising god was first raised by James Frazer (1854-1941) in his seminal work 'The Golden Bough,' with the dying and rising therein associated with the fertility rites surrounding the yearly cycle of vegetation. The gods Frazer identified as fitting this pattern were Osiris, Tammuz, Adonis, Attis, Dionysus, Ishtar and Persephone. I don't wish to explore these stories in too detailed a manner, as they are all easily accessible, but still a quick survey will indicate some of the similarities, though also, as we shall see, the differences with the biblical story of the dying and rising of the Divine in Jesus. These stories often come in different forms to us, often unclear especially in the forms they developed, contemporaneous with Jesus, as Mystery cults. Given, they were mysteries revealed only to initiates we would clearly expect such secrecy.

The Osiris myth was the most elaborate and influential story in ancient Egyptian mythology, having exceptional antiquity, reaching its basic form in or before the 24th century BCE. The myth tells of the murder of the god Osiris, a primeval king of Egypt, and its consequences. Osiris is murdered by his brother Set or Seth, who after cutting his body into pieces, usurps his throne, this throwing the realm into chaos. Isis, the consort of Osiris, along with Nethys, in like relationship to Set, begins a search for the body of Osiris. After much searching the goddesses find and restore Osiris's body with the help of other deities, including Throth the god of healing, so possessing also great magical powers, and Anubis, the god associated with embalming and funerary rites. Osiris then becomes the first mummy, the gods' efforts to restore his body being the mythological basis for Egyptian embalming practices, which sought to prevent and reverse the decay following death. Isis completes the restoration of her husband's body, allowing him to posthumously conceive a son, Horus with her, who becomes Set's rival for the throne, their violent conflict ending with Horus' triumph, with a resultant restoration of order to Egypt following Set's chaotic reign. This elevation to the throne completes the process of Osiris' resurrection. The story was central to Egyptian understanding, especially in its concern for order, 'maat,' that order guaranteed by royal succession, which of clearly the story also legitimises. Disorder is evidenced by death and subsequent decay, so this story is also about overcoming that disruption, t h r o u g h providing a means to eternal life. While individual pharaohs die, the Pharaoh as divine never dies, and while Pharaoh reigns an unchanging order prevails. Egyptian religion is all about maintenance of the sacred order, with the dying and rising god in Egypt having its goal, the justification of that order.

This would be the order from which the Hebrew slaves rebelled, though the Hebrew tradition also had a strong concern for order, evidenced in the opening chapters of Genesis, where God brings order out of chaos. That order, however, is limited to the cosmological domain, and does not extend as ideological justification to the human economic and social order.

The other great cultural centre in the Ancient Near East was that domain situated in modern day Iraq, those civilisations which succeeded each other in Mesopotamia, the area between the Tigrus and Euphrates rivers – the Sumerians, Akkadians, Babylonians and Assyrians. Though each empire succeeded its predecessor by defeating it, each inherited their predecessor's mythology with the gods being fairly constant, though taking different names, with Innana for instance becoming Ishtar, while many of the mythological stories, central to understanding the roles of the gods were maintained in gradually re-worked forms, the best known being the Epic of Gilgamesh.

The one known as Dumuzi to the Sumerians, later as Tammuz, was worshipped successively in Sumeria, Akkad, Assyria and Babylonia, his name even being present, not favourably in the Hebrew Scriptures. (Ezek 8:14-15) He was another dying and rising god, and in that he was joined by his consort, in Sumeria called Innana, later, as just seen, better known as Ishtar. In this myth cycle we have a story where, as often seen, the actions of the gods determine the fertility of the land, it being dry while the fertility god or goddess is absent in the never-world but springing to life when the divine one returns. There are several variations of the Damuzi/Tammuz story, with the textual evidence often not clear. In some versions it is Tammuz who dies, sometimes even killed by Ishtar, who then travels to the underworld to retrieve and revive him. In other cases it is Ishtar who is taken, with Tammuz being the one who must seek her out. Whatever the case it was held that the onset of the hot dry period following the summer solstice, marked the time when it was believed that Ishtar was in the underworld. Passing through seven gates in the descent Ishtar is progressively stripped bare, the items removed symbolic of the stripping of her powers, whereupon arriving she is killed by her sister Ereshkigal, resident there, who then hangs her on a stake. A deal is struck with Ereshkigal, that deal allowing Ishtar to be resurrected back to the earth for six months each year, those months being the months of the earth's fertility. During that six months Tammuz, sometimes his sister Geshtinana, takes Ishtar's place in that subterranean abode.

The myth of the Greek dying and rising god Adonis is of similar type. Adonis was a most handsome youth loved by both Aphrodite and Persephone, the latter being the goddess of the underworld. Aphrodite left Adonis in the care of Persephone who took him for her lover. Jealous of this, Aphrodite demanded that Persephone hand him over to her, which she refused. Finally Zeus was forced to intervene, awarding Adonis to Aphrodite for six months of the year and Persephone for the other six months. The time Adonis was in the underworld with Persephone coincided with the dry season, the earth lacking fertility, while the return to the earth by Adonis brought the reviving rains. Adonis' death and resurrection, symbolic of this vegetal cycle, was widely celebrated in ancient Greece in the festival of Adonia, held mid-summer.

Persephone, also known as Kore, was herself another dying and rising goddess, closely associated with the agricultural cycle. She was the daughter of Zeus and Demeter, the goddess of the harvest, but was abducted by Hades, the god of the underworld. This caused the distraught Demeter to scour the earth seeking her, thereby neglecting her role as goddess of the harvest, resulting in a famine, before she is told by the all-seeing sun Helios that Persephone had been snatched by Hades. Zeus having been assailed by the cries of the hungry populace and of the other deities finally forces Hades to return Persephone. Hades releases her, but not before giving her some pomegranate seeds which she eats, meaning she must spend the winter months in the underworld from which she emerges each spring. She finally became queen of the underworld and death, and as such is often found depicted upon sarcophagi, being the one after-all, whom the underworld cannot keep.

The Phrygian Attis is yet another case of the dying and rising god associated with the vegetal cycle. Attis was either the lover or son of the fertility goddess Cybele, who on learning of his being unfaithful with a nymph killed the nymph, whereupon Attis was driven to such madness that he castrated himself, slowly bleeding to death. His death caused the crops to not grow, causing the gods to decide to resurrect him each spring, so as to ensure the earth's fertility. The dying and rising Attis symbolises the fruits of the earth, which after dying in the winter, rise again in the spring.

Many particularly identify the Greek god Dionysus most closely with Jesus. Dionysus, like Jesus, is born of a union between the divine and a mortal, in this case Zeus with Semele. Hera, the consort of Zeus, jealous of his infidelity, has the Titans tear Dionysius apart. The stories vary, but Athena, Demeter or Rhea, one of the Titans, manages to save Dionysus' heart. Zeus then places that heart upon his thigh and recreates him guaranteeing his protection. By such it was held that Dionysus was twice-born. Having been killed and then re-born resurrected, he becomes one of the very few who was able to bring a person back to life following their death. Not only 'twice-born' and resurrected and the gateway through which his adherents can gain eternal life, but also associated with wine along with being a divine one, who is also experienced rather than just being formally worshipped, Dionysus has a number of connections with Jesus. Further Dionysus was also celebrated by a ritual meal of bread and wine.

In the above stories it is interesting to find just how often resurrection takes place on the third day. Osiris dies 17th Athys (November) and is revived on the 19th. Attis' death takes place 22nd March with his return to life being probably 25th March, while Adonis was most likely resurrected on the third day.

It is argued that Judaism, which primarily shapes the Jesus story, was little influenced by such ideas but if this is so, how do we explain the Jewish revolt concerning Greek thinking and culture, particularly by the nationalist Maccabees against the Seleucids in the second century BCE? Given that major revolt, it is clear that Greek influences must have been extensive in Israel. During the time of the Seleucid occupation Jewish practices such as circumcision and Sabbath observance, things at the heart of their faith were forbidden on the pain of death. Greek influences such as the gymnasium also found their place in Israel. We know that at that time Jewish men participated in the gymnasium even trying to reverse the sign of their circumcision, while many also attended the theatre. We are told that the immediate stimulus for the revolt was the bringing of pagan objects into the temple. (1 Macc 1:54, 59) Quite clearly pagan influences were prevalent in Israel. So widely practiced were they there was a popular revolt raised against them.

In other parts of the world, from very distinct religious traditions we also find the pattern of a dying and rising god. The best known comes from India, where in the Hindu tradition Shiva kills the god, Ganesha by cutting off his head, but when faced with an irate Parvati, Shiva's wife and Ganesha's mother, replaces the severed head with that most handy, that of an elephant, and thereby brings Ganesha back to life. I am not claiming there is any historical connection with this last story, though Greek Indian contact was not unknown with Alexander the Great having travelled to India, but rather am using it to show that there is perhaps what Carl Jung would call an archetypal belief represented by the idea of a dying and rising god.

In the above stories there are numerous similarities to Jesus as the dying and rising divine one. Ishtar being stripped bare is somewhat reminiscent of how, as we have seen, Paul understands the kenosis of Christ in Philippians 2:5-11. Further, her being hung on a stake mirrors that of Jesus' end. The self-castration by Attis may have some connection with Jesus' call to be 'eunuchs for the kingdom,' (Matt 19:12) while the association with Persephone, returned from the underworld as had Jesus, makes both eminently suitable to be displayed as sarcophagi. We have just of course, examined the Dionysus/Jesus links.

These similarities, however, are hardly overwhelming. Even a cursory reading will show that these above described stories are clearly distinct from that which Christians understand as describing the dying and rising divine one, Jesus. The above accounts have no historicity nor do they have any interest in making historical claims, all clearly being in the realm of mythology. The adherents of these gods thus participated in their resurrection by ritual cultic means. Jesus' resurrection, on the other hand, is located historically, held to be due to historical causes. He is understood as being judged and condemned by the authorities for the nature of his ministry, and the challenge it represented, meaning Jesus' death and resurrection has an ethical dimension associated with it. Even the resurrection is presented as having a historicity about it. As said, this lack of historical interest and location does not make these other stories any less important for the truth they are speaking is in another, though no less important domain, myth. It is, however, a clearly different domain, with these myths and the Jesus story belonging to a different type of literature. This is not to say, however, as we shall see, that mythological motifs do not get attached to the Jesus story, especially that part of it to do with the resurrection.

Lest I be accused of providing an apologetic in defense of the Christian story as opposed to these others, I again point out that in deep essence an historical action carries neither more, nor less import than that experienced in the domain of mythology. Indeed it may be the latter which is more effective.

Given this difference, I do not believe therefore that the dying-and-rising god motif can explain the origin of the notion of Christ's resurrection among his earliest followers, though it almost certainly played a significant role in contributing to the later spread and popularity of Christianity in the Roman empire. It is perhaps even possible to see the early stages of that transformation of Jesus from being Jewish Messiah, to the dying and rising god more common in the wider Greco-Roman cultural milieu in the biblical writings of both Paul and John.

Let us now turn from the pagan domain to examine the belief in resurrection more closely from within that Jewish context which of most shaped Jesus and the early Christian writers. What traditionally had been the Jewish understanding of resurrection, and how had it developed by the time of Jesus?

Chapter Two

Sheol's shadow to dry bones rising

Before turning to the Christian testimony concerning the resurrection we need to clearly first examine the background beliefs of that community from which the resurrection testimony arose. That background for all the very earliest believers, and indeed all the writers of the Christian Scriptures, with the possible exception of Luke, was Jewish, so we need therefore to examine both the traditional and contemporary Jewish beliefs in the resurrection? I say both traditional and contemporary, for just prior to the time of Jesus, during the inter-testamental period, attitudes and belief toward resurrection had undergone major change.

There are a range of responses within the Hebrew Scriptures to the question, 'If mortals die will they rise again?' (Job 14:14) Nowhere, however, in these Scriptures do we find the confirmatory answer to that question which we find in the Christian Scriptures. Sometimes they made the brutal assessment that having breathed your last, you no longer had any existence, either understood as returning to dust, (Gen 3:19, Ps 90:3) or the grave, (Gen 37:35, Is 14:11) while at other times death was understood not as extinction, but rather as a continued existence in the underworld. Where such existence was predicated beyond death, it was not something to which one looked forward, but rather represented a nebulous existence in an ethereal world, Sheol, of half shadows, misery and futility. (Job 26:5, Ps 88:10, Prov 9:18, Isa 26:14) As such there was dread regarding the approach of this nothingness in death, and therefore petition for God's protection from it. (Psalm 39, especially verse 13) That fear of death arose primarily because, it was believed the concern of the divine, understood as the God of life, did not extend to that place, (Ps 6:5, 30:9, 88:5, 10-12) and because from such a place there could be no hope then of deliverance. (Ps 16:10) To be in Sheol was to be cut off from one's family and community as well as from God, for the dead were not able to return to the earth, (2 Sam 12:23) except by necromancy, (1 Sam 2:6, 1 Sam 28: 1-25) with that practice being strongly condemned (Deut 18:9-11, Isa 8:19).

Though the well-known Psalm 139:8 claims, that even in Sheol God is present, that statement would seem to be more an doxological or exultatory claim as to the omnipresence of God, than one made in a reflective theological manner.

Jacob on hearing of what he supposes to be his son Joseph's death speaks of going to Sheol to search for him, (Gen 37:35) but this again speaks more of the existential pain of his loss, than what was the theological appropriate thing to do, and as such testifies eloquently of that pain he feels for his lost son.

To die was to either be extinguished, or to irreversibly enter Sheol and endure a shadowy existence cut off from God defined as life, with there being but one doorway between Sheol and earthly existence, death, through which there was no return. That desolate place called 'Sheol' or the 'pit' was later translated into Greek as 'Hades.'

There are responses, of course, which are different to the norm within the Hebrew Scriptures. One of those comes from the same book, Job, from which comes that question with which we begun, as to whether mortals having died shall rise again. Here is affirmed that following the death of one who it is said after his 'skin has thus been destroyed, then apart from my flesh, I shall see God whom I shall see on my side.' (Job 19:25-27) This is part of one of Job's responses to his inquisitors, and again sounds more a doxological statement affirming Job's trust in God in the face of the inquisitor's challenge, than one confirming a well-thought theological position as regards existence after death. To that question from this book which we are examining, Job theologically affirms the traditional belief, 'a person lies down and rises not again, till the heavens are no more he will not awake or be roused out of his sleep... but the mountain falls and crumbles away and the rock is removed from its place; the waters wear away the stones; the torrents wash away the soil of the earth, so you destroy human hope... His sons come to honor and he does not know it; they are brought low and he perceives it not. He feels only the pain of his own body, and he mourns only for himself.' (Job 14:12-21) Clearly there is no resurrection but rather a long suffering endurance in Sheol which has no attractiveness about it, nor knowledge concerning the things on earth. The deceased in this case feeling the pain of their own body, knows nothing of the honor or otherwise of their children.

Though in the Psalms we find the Psalmist speaking of how, in contradistinction to those who place their trust in riches, 'God will ransom my soul from the power of Sheol, for he will receive me,' (Ps 49:15) the context makes clear the rescue from Sheol being spoken, is the prolongation of the petitioner's life, not some rescue following their death from such place. In this Psalm the actual theological understanding of death is summed up in the final verse, 'Humans cannot abide in their pomp, they are like the beasts that perish.' (Ps 49:20)

Within the 'Suffering Servant' songs one particular verse is of interest. In Isaiah 53:12 we read the words, 'He will see his off-spring and prolong his days.' There has been much debate around the meaning of these suffering servant songs found in Deutero-Isaiah (the extended Isaianic tradition, some 150-200 years after the original component of that book, thus the term, 'deutero' meaning second), with much of that debate centered on whether the songs refer to some individual whose suffering is somehow, and it is never explained how, redemptive, or whether it is the suffering of Israel itself which is redemptive. In either case the clear intention here apropos 'prolong his days,' reflects the core Jewish concern of having offspring so that one's name 'may continue in the land,' (Deut 31:13, 2 Chron 6:31) as one lived on by one's name living on. As such resurrection or resuscitation in the Hebrew Scriptures is used metaphorically of the nation as a whole or of a person living on through their sons, it always being, in such a patriarchal society, sons rather than daughters. Of the first, the best known case is the valley of dry bones in Ezekiel. In this instance we are again clearly not in the place of literal resurrection, the passage itself making clear that this is a 'vision' of Ezekiel, (Ezek 37:1-14) nor are we speaking of individual resurrection, given reference to national revival is being clearly made.

Only a few passages from the Hebrew Scriptures seemingly speak of life after death being more real than Sheol's shadowy existence. The first of these is Isaiah 25:8, 'God will swallow up death forever' (used by Paul to argue for the resurrection in 1 Corinthians 15:54), but clearly the context of this again makes it clear that which is being spoken of is corporate 'resurrection,' understood as the revival and elevation of Israel with all nations coming to Mount Zion to share in a great eschatological feast imaged as 'richest food and finest wine.' Given this clearly different context to individual resurrection these words should be understood allegorically, that Israel no longer will suffer death at the hands of oppressors. These particular words could also be a later interpolation into the text in that they so differ from the surrounding thought. This leads to some scholars assigning them to a late place, dates varying between the 3rd and 2nd century B.C.E. If that late date is correct then it is quite possible, as we shall see, that a reference to individual resurrection beyond the grave is being made. In the next chapter we find, 'Those of our people who have died will live again! Their bodies will come back to life, all those sleeping in their graves will wake up and sing for joy. As the sparkling dew refreshes the earth, so the Lord will revive those who have long been dead.' (Isa 26:19) Again the context in which these words are found is clearly different, these words standing in sharp contrast to the prevailing sentiment, where the writer is clearly speaking of life and death metaphorically, to do with the nation Israel. Again this reference to revival for the nation could have led a later scribe to re-interpret the passage to give it reference to individual resurrection. When speaking unambiguously of the individual the writer maintains the orthodox view, 'they are dead, they will not live; they are shades, they will not arise.' (Isa 26:14) Isaiah seems actually to be strongly making his plea to God to deliver Israel in light of such understanding, for deliverance can only come this side of the grave, for beyond it, in accord with the orthodox view, there can be no deliverance.

In the book of Hosea we find the words which may well have had some influence on the gospel resurrection accounts, 'after two days he will revive us; on the third day he will raise us up that we may live before him.' (Hos 6:2). Again, however, the context makes it very clear that here national revival rather than individual resurrection is meant. Hosea's attitude is most clearly an implied no to the question he poses, 'Shall I ransom them from the power of Sheol? Shall I redeem them from death.' (Hos 13:14) A reading of the context will clearly show that, God in judgment is actually looking for Sheol and plagues so to to put an end to Israel's rebellion. While there may be national revival, the idea of an individual existence beyond the grave is completely unknown to Hosea.

Only two figures from the Hebrew Scriptural story escape death as their fate. The first is Enoch, (Gen 5:24) the other, Israel's greatest prophet, Elijah. (2 Kgs 2:9-11) Nothing, however, is made of this regarding their individual survival beyond the grave in the Hebrew Scriptures themselves, but by the time of the inter-testamental writings these two figures become increasingly used to prove that the grave is not the end for all. Many will know of such use made in the Christian story, where Elijah is available, having not died, to make an appearance in the Transfiguration. (Mk 9:2-8 and pars) The other figure who appears in that story is Moses, and in a sense he was held to have transcended the grave in that, 'no one knows the place of his burial to this day.' (Deut 3:6, 34:6) The document 'The Assumption of Moses' is from around the Christian era, and as the name implies Moses was believed to have been taken straight to the heavens. The Jewish tradition speaks of the Archangel Michael disputing with Satan for the body of Moses. Assuming the former won, it appears that there is a tradition that Israel's great law-giver, like its greatest prophet was likewise taken directly to heaven.[1] A whole inter-testamental tradition is built around Enoch, especially found in the book bearing his name.

Only one passage from the Hebrew Scriptures unambiguously affirms life beyond the grave. From Daniel we read, 'Many who sleep in the dust of the Earth will awake, some to everlasting life, others to shame and everlasting contempt.' (Dan 12:2). A few verses later a promise is made, 'at the end of your days you will rise to receive your allotted inheritance.' (Dan 12:13) The book of Daniel is almost universally dated to the Maccabean time around 165 BCE, very late in the Hebrew Scriptural tradition, from a time when individual resurrection was increasingly becoming a part of the Jewish understanding. Interestingly the idea of universal resurrection is spoken of here whereby both the righteous and the unrighteous would be raised to reward and condemnation, with the latter entering Gehenna. Whereas Sheol was a neutral place of abode Gehenna had altogether darker connotations, for it was there that one was judged by God amid the flames. Gehenna was associated with the Valley of Himmon, just to the south of Jerusalem, a place where child sacrifices as offerings to the god Moloch had been carried out. The area having such an unsavory association was used as the city's garbage tip from where clearly we get our image of the everlasting fires of Hell. The idea of a shadowy existence in Sheol has here been replaced with life beyond the grave, something far more concrete, either in eternal bliss or torment.

---

[1] Midrash Deut. Rabbah xi. 6

Having entered the Hebrew Scriptural tradition at its very conclusion, belief in the resurrection of the individual continued to grow in the inter-testamental period, to the extent that by the time of Jesus it was popularly held. We can find an example of that development in comparing the book of Sirach, also known as Ecclesiasticus, from the early part of the 2nd century BCE wherein we find the words affirming the traditional view that, 'at death a person abides in Sheol, a place of unending sleep,' (Sirach 30:17, 46:19) a place of silence, (Sirach 17:17-28) with immortality being restricted to the nation and the enduring nature of a person's good name, (Sirach 37:26, 39:9, 44:8-15) to the attitude of a later writing, 'The Wisdom of Solomon,' (2nd-1st century BCE) which takes a much more affirmative view concerning life beyond the grave claiming that, 'the righteous find peace and incorruptible existence.' (Wisd of Sol 2:23, 5:5, 6:19)

Views as to the nature of the resurrection, whether it was for all or just the righteous, and it being physical or spiritual in form, also varied in the inter-testamental period. Thus, in the book of Enoch, a work scholars believe was compiled over a period of time from the third century BCE to the first century CE there are, as we would expect given that extensive time frame, a whole range of views to do with resurrection. A physical resurrection is emphasized in 1 Enoch 92: 35, 104: 2, 4, but in 103:4 we learn that rather than a physical resurrection it is 'in their spirits' that they will live and rejoice but not perish. This later passage would seem to be evidence of the increasing Hellenist influence entering Jewish thought at the time. The tension between the newer Hellenist influence entering Judaism with its dualist body/spirit or body/soul separation, and the traditional holistic view of the human evident in the Jewish tradition, is also caught up in the variance of views concerning the physicality of the resurrection in the books of Maccabees. Thus in writing of 'the seven martyrs' the older tradition found in 2 Maccabees speaks of a physical resurrection while that which is newer, 4 Maccabees, substitutes immortality of the soul for physical. (2 Macc 7:14 cf 4 Macc 9:22, 10:15, 16:13, 18:23) Indeed the physicality of the resurrection is understood very literally in the earlier tradition in 2 Maccabees 7:10, 11, 17-46, where of the seven martyrs it is said they will rise with their missing body parts, taken under torture, restored to them. This literal understanding of the resurrection almost certainly lay behind the practice within Judaism of burial rather than cremation for the latter did not allow for anything to be left in order to be resurrected. This literal understanding is almost certainly behind Jesus saying, 'if your hand or your foot causes you to sin, cut it off and throw it away; it is better for you to enter life maimed or lame than with two hands or two feet to be thrown into the eternal fire. And if your eye causes you to sin, pluck it out and throw it away; it is better for you to enter life with one eye than with two eyes to be thrown into the hell (lit. Gehenna) of fire.' (Matt 18:8-9) The limbs, according to this view, would be restored post-resurrection anyway. Of Jesus himself we are told that, unlike the case for many during crucifixion, his legs were unbroken. (John 19:33) This would serve to present him unblemished in the next life. To have blemish in antiquity was understood to have sin attached to oneself.

It was the suffering endured by many, including the seven martyrs, along with many others such as Razias, (2 Macc 14:37-46, esp. the last verse) at the hands of the Hellenist Seleucids, which almost certainly gave powerful stimulus to the idea of personal resurrection. The seeds of such views as individual resurrection are almost certainly found in the Babylonian exile, and the continuing influence of Babylonian thought on Judaism, given the vast Jewish community opting to remain in that city following the return from exile.[2]

At the core of this Babylonian influence was the Zoroastrian religion, the earliest of all religions to have a judgment of both the righteous and the evil, with that judgment framed by ethics. Zoroastrianism was the religion of the Persian Empire for over 1,000 years, and it came to greatly influence Judaism, Christianity and even the religion which eventually supplanted it, Islam. Zoroastrianism centered on a monotheistic supreme being Ahura Mazda, identified with the good order of creation, who was opposed by a devil-like figure of chaos, Angra Mainyu.[3] A person had free will to live to the good or the evil, and following death was raised to judgment

---

[2] The Babylonian Talmud (Talmud Bavli) was more highly regarded than that of Jerusalem (Talmud Yerushalmi).

[3] Zorosatrianism originated in Persia its roots going back perhaps as early as the 2nd millenium BCE, entering recorded history c. 500 BCE. It was the state religion of pre-Islamic Persia from 600 BCE to 650 CE. It is marked by dualism and eschatological monotheism. Adherents follow the teachings of the Iranian prophet Zoroaster or Zarathustra. The Supreme Being is known as Ahura Mazda and is opposed by an evil Angra Mainyu. A number of its characteristics, such as messianism, heaven and hell, free will, and therefore ethical responsibility, have influenced other religious systems, including Judaism, Christianity, and Islam.

in accord to how ethically they had lived their life. The image used was a narrow bridge, called the Chinvat, spanned across a chasm which would be successfully traversed by the virtuous, but not so by those who lived unethically, who would fall to the flames burning in the great chasm below. Just this very brief examination of Zoroastrianism is sufficient to indicate how powerfully it came to shape Judaism leading up to the time of Jesus and then clearly into Christian, and Islamic, understandings of, among other things, those central to our examination, the nature and purpose of resurrection, and an individual being raised and judged in accord with their ethical living.

The development of the idea of individual resurrection to eternal life or everlasting punishment found great stimulus in the often harsh Seleucid actions carried out on the colonized Jewish nation. The Seleucids, successors to the Alexandrian empire, ruled in a particularly brutal manner. The suffering of the righteous under such a regime clearly gave lie to the old view that God rewarded the good, while punishing the evil in this life. From such realization arose the theological view that though many of the righteous may be suffering now, at the eschaton they would be raised to receive their vindication and reward. God's providence, missing in the current state of things, would come then in a future existence in another domain following death, where that divine retributive justice, clearly not taking place in the present, would be exercised, with the vindicated virtuous receiving their reward of eternal life, while the evil would receive the punishment which was their due. This served to preserve God's righteousness, literally theodicy, for how could God be righteous if it was the evil who prospered while the good suffered? With resurrection to judgment resulting in reward or punishment for individuals, this awkward conundrum could be resolved.

The two stimuli then, the influence of Zoroastrianism and the Seleucid oppression, serve as root causes leading to Judaism developing the idea of individual resurrection, either to reward or fiery torment. Still, however, resurrection was restricted to those within Judaism.

The idea of universal resurrection of both the righteous and unrighteous is first found in (4 Ezra 4:41-43, 7:32-38, Testament of Benjamin 10:6-9, 2 Apocalypse of Baruch 49:2 – 51:12, 85:13). Here, rather than just the Jews, people of all nations are called into judgment before Israel's God. This is associated with the movement away from henotheism, the idea that while Israel's God was their only god, a type of tribal god who didn't negate the existence of other gods for other tribes, to the idea of monotheism, that Israel's God was the only God, the universal God for all peoples, who finally would come streaming from all over the earth to worship on Mount Zion.

This universal resurrection however, was not the position taken by all with some believing in restricting such to righteous Israelites only. (1 Enoch 22:13,46:6, 51:1-2, Psalms of Solomon 3:11-16, 13:9-11, 14:4- 10, 15:12-15) That position is clearly understandable given the context in which resurrection belief arose, as response to the suffering of the Jewish people, the specificity of that framing the more narrow response. Given that resurrection was a form of retributive justice for God's people, oppressed in their earthly existence, why would it be extended to those of other lands, to those foreigners who were oppressing them?

There was, however, a further stimulus to belief in individual resurrection in the latter part of the inter-testmental period, that being the widespread dissemination and popularity of the 'mystery cults'. These were popular forms of religious observance outside, but also alongside, the official Roman cult. There were many of these usually with their origins in the common religious forms in the Indo- European and Indo-Iranian worlds; the Eleusinian, the Dionysian and the Orphic Mysteries being the best known. The cult of Mithraism, centered on the Persian God Mithra, in which initiates were bathed in the blood of a bull, a link to fertility and virility, was especially important. Mithraism over time represented the major challenge to Christianity for dominance in the empire. These mystery cults represented developments out of the myths upon which I touched in the previous chapter, and they became increasingly important in the centuries preceding Jesus. As the term implies these were secret cults, only initiates sharing in the mysteries, such secrecy clearly restricting our intimately knowing them. We do know however, they were mostly built around the idea of a dying and rising god with initiates, through teaching and rituals, sharing in that dying and rising.

The Eleusinian cult, forms of which go back at least to the 6th century BCE, was probably the most widely practiced, being so for the best part of a millennium. At its core was the sharing in the death and resurrection of Persephone or Kore, daughter of Demeter. We have seen how this myth gave explication to the months of fertility, but also of barrenness. It increasingly became linked to an individual's rising and subsequent resurrection.

As pointed out earlier Judaism, and thus clearly Christianity, was not immune to these pagan influences.

In conclusion, we have seen that through the inter-testamental period there was a wider acceptance over time of individual resurrection as being something real as distinct from such being used as a metaphor only for familial posterity or national revival. That belief in individual resurrection, stimulated by questions concerning theodicy, the preservation of divine righteousness in the face of Seleucid persecution of the righteous, along with the influence of Zoroastrianism, and also links with the Mystery Cults, continued to grow through the inter-testamental period, so that by the time of Jesus resurrection was largely accepted as Jewish orthodoxy being held by the vast majority of the Jewish populace. Sheol as a nebulous abode for all, dreaded due to it being beyond God's providential care, became replaced by judgment either to life or condemnation, meted out first of all to Jewish believers, but then to all. Belief in resurrection, though there were differences in understanding, became ever more universal as we move through the inter- testamental period to the time of Jesus. Let us now turn to that epoch.

Chapter Three

The grave transcended

By the time we arrive at the age of Jesus, individual resurrection and judgment to either perdition or glory, had become almost universally held. In Acts we find assumed that Paul can even speak of the resurrection before the Jewish king Agrippa without any reticence. (Acts 26: 23) To the charge made against him that he is 'mad' Paul responds that he has said nothing, including reference to resurrection, that Agrippa would not have known and accepted.

Indeed so popular and accepted had it become, it seems necessary for the gospel writers to remind their readers that there are some who didn't hold to it! Luke takes it as being self-evident from within the tradition of 'Moses and the prophets.' (Luke 24:21, 26-27, 32, 44-46, Acts 26:22) Generally only those viewed as rooted in the tradition as the Sadducees, rejected it. (Matthew 22:23, Mark 12:18-27, Acts 23:8, 26:8, Josephus Antiquities 18:14) They may have had little need of it for their wealthy earthly life was such, they were already largely living in a state of bliss.

Resurrection was understood to be to 'paradise,' a term derived from Persian for a garden, particularly one which was well manicured with pools, fountains, and other such features. Such gardens belonged to the wealthy and the Sadducees, possessing gardens of 'paradise,' had less need than others to seek paradise elsewhere. Given their 'blessed' existence, the Sadducees were quite comfortable holding to the conservative tradition, with its lack of anything to do with individual resurrection, save a shadowy existence in Sheol. The Sadducees represented a minority in Israel, and Paul on trial before the Sanhedrin seeks to divide it along its Sadducee/Pharisee party line, by testifying to the resurrection. So sharp was the division that he was apparently successful in so doing. (Acts 23:1-10)

Despite the widespread acceptance of resurrection, there was much diversity of thought as to what that actually entailed. To that diversity I now turn.

The Pharisees, though they too were interpreters of the tradition, were prepared to take on board the idea of a resurrection and eternal age to come, which would only exclude the apostates, who they believed would be raised, but to judgment. (Acts 23:6-8) Some of the Pharisees Josephus charges, even believed in reincarnation.[1] Many of the Pharisaical schools had developed in the Seleucid period in reaction to the syncretist tendencies of large numbers of the Jewish populace. Refusing such compromise with the Seleucids they suffered, many being martyred at the hands of that cruel empire. As already explored, it made sense for them to develop the idea of individual resurrection, as a compensatory solution to the injustice meted out to them in this life.

The view of the Essenes is unclear based on the evidence of the Dead Sea Scrolls (and I take the majority view that they were the authors and keepers of the scrolls), where statements referring to their 'habitation with the angels' could be taken to be reference to their current exalted existence, or refer to something future beyond the grave. (1 QS 'The Community Rule' 2:25, I QH 'Thanksgiving Hymns' 3:19-23, 11:10-14) It is likely however that the Essenes, like the Pharisees, also excluded from power, looked to the resurrection as a means by which God would right the current wrongs. As to the nature of their resurrection understanding, Josephus speaks of the Essenes as believing in 'the immortality of the soul,' (Josephus: Jewish War 8:1-2, 11) contrary to Hippolytus, (170-235 CE) who later speaks of them also believing in a physical resurrection. Hippolytus, as a Christian, may have an interest in having the Essenes hold such a belief, for physical resurrection, understood very literally by that time, had become Christian orthodoxy.

The views held by these three schools probably owe as much if not more to their political status in Israel than any metaphysical reason. The Sadducees, as seen, were satisfied with the current order of which they were beneficiaries, and would have understood resurrection as judgment on that order, in that it would indicate God's righteous satisfaction wasn't complete in this world, justice needing to be satisfied in another. Both the Pharisees and Essenes were marginalized groups from a power, of which they were highly critical. They saw resurrection as a means of retributive

---

[1] The Pharisees say that all souls are incorruptible; but that the souls of good men are only removed into other bodies; --- but that the souls of bad men are subject to eternal punishment. Josephus, Wars of the Jews II.Viii.14.

Chapter Three: The grave transcended

justice, in which the current wrong would be righted by divine intervention on their behalf.

In saying this, it should be pointed out that resurrection in all its variance, was always understood as being more than merely an individual's survival beyond the grave. The older traditional view of resurrection as national revival continued to inform all understandings, meaning that it became something to be understood as vindication not only for the righteousness of an individual, but also that of the nation, and even the grouping itself, be it the Pharisees or Essenes. Further, the idea of the survival of the familial line through one's male produce continued to be important right through the Jewish community, with the exception of those very few, linked with the Essenes, who lived celibate lives.[2]

At the other extreme to views of resurrection held by Sadducees, were those held by the radically marginalized, those understanding themselves as having absolutely no stake in the existing order of things. From that perspective, they understood the resurrection as a very literal reversal of the current order; a type of retributive justice, in which they as the oppressed would be vindicated, such vindication often being crudely understood as their coming rule over those who had repressed them. The type of resurrection was embodied, and thus resurrected they would act as the agents of the Divine 'clean up' of the earth, ridding it of its evildoers and oppressors, with God leading them in this task of apocalyptic cleansing. This type of philosophy underpinned the thought of such millennial insurrectionist groups associated with rebellious figures, such as Theudas, Judas the Galilean, 'the Egyptian', John the Baptist, and probably the majority of those who followed Jesus into Jerusalem that day, just five days before his execution.

Our examination of the Jewish context, from which of course Jesus comes, has shown that among the various groupings there were a plethora of views regarding the nature of the resurrection. The genesis of the idea found in Zoroastrianism, received it's great stimulus in Israel during the time of Seleucid oppression, and subsequently having grown in reaction to foreign domination, later found itself ironically increasingly influenced in the forms it took by foreign influences, notably that body/soul dualism carried by Greek thought. Resurrection had as its location sometimes this

---

[2] Pliny the Elder, Historia Naturalis V, 17 or 29, Josephus, The Wars of the Jews 2.119

earth, other times a transformed earth, or to an extra-terrestrial place called paradise. It either took place in the body, in a transformed body, or sometimes, where Greek ideas were more prevalent, as a soul without body.

It was from this varied context that Jesus was to draw his ideas concerning resurrection, and we will find that this variety makes its way both into Jesus' ideas concerning resurrection and his practice. It is to him we now turn.

Chapter Four

Jesus' understanding and practice

The Christian Scriptures claim that Jesus believed in the resurrection, while also claiming that such belief is founded upon the Hebrew Scriptural tradition. Thus, so it was claimed by the resurrected Christ himself on opening the disciples 'minds to understand the Scriptures,' that 'thus it is written, that the Christ should suffer and on the third day rise from the dead.' (Luke 24:46, 1 Cor 15:4) It is most difficult to find any Hebrew Scripture, as already seen, which makes this clear. The nearest we can find is Hosea 6:2 which, as we have seen, in speaking of being 'raised up' on the third day is clearly referencing the community of Israel. Perhaps the infant church felt it legitimate to use such a passage referring to a community and apply it to an individual, given that it viewed Christ as the raiser of a new Israel, namely the church. (Rom 4: 9-25) While Isaiah 53:10, part of the best known of the 'suffering servant songs' in the latter tradition of the Isaianic school (Deutero-Isaiah), speaks of this suffering servant, noting that, 'he shall prolong his days,' strangely enough, this passage is not ever used as a proof text in the Christian Scriptures. Other passages are usable, and indeed are used, but to us their use has little conviction. Ps 16:8-11 (used in Acts 2:25-28), Ps 110:1 (Acts 2:34), Ps 118:22 (Acts 4:11).

None of these, except the reference from Hosea, gives us the third day 'proof' demanded by both Luke and Paul. Concerning the three days Matthew makes use of the Jonah story, whereby the prophet was swallowed by the great fish for 'three days and three nights,' (Jonah 1:17) to have Jesus say that likewise he will 'three days and three nights in the heart of the earth,' (Matt 12:40) and having him make a link of the signs he gives to that of the 'sign of Jonah,' charging just as Jonah was a sign to those in Nineveh, so will the 'son of man' be to those of his generation. Unlike the sign of Jonah to Nineveh, however, which was accepted, and brought repentance, (Jon 3:6-10) that of the Son of man shall not be thus received. Given this episode is not present in Mark, it seems that both Matthew and Luke are drawing on the same source, that known by scholars as Q. To Q I shall return later. Interestingly Luke, while using the rest of the pericope from where the material is being drawn, does not speak of the three days and three nights, perhaps finding it problematical in that Jesus was not three days and nights 'in the belly of the earth.' It is interesting to note that Luke holds little enough worth in that story, as a pointer to the resurrection, so as to use it to make a completely different point. (Luke 11: 29-32) In any case the idea that Jesus actually spoke of his coming death as eschatological judgement seems improbable. We can conclude that these words, supposedly from the mouth of Jesus, look far more like creations of a post-resurrection church.

Last to do with the three days there is a possible shaping of the Matthean tradition of Jesus' resurrection appearance on the mountain in Galilee from Exodus: 'Go to the people and consecrate them today and tomorrow, and let them wash their garments, and be ready by the third day; for on the third day the Lord will come down upon Mount Sinai in the sight of all the people.' (Ex 19:10) None of this, however, is terribly convincing to our ears. We can conclude, there is nothing in the Hebrew Scriptures which points to the resurrection of an individual like Jesus. As we have earlier noted, resurrection belief was barely present in the Hebrew Scriptures, only touched upon in their latest writings, largely finding its genesis in the inter-testamental era.

Given, however, the method of midrash common to the Jewish tradition, it was essential for the gospel writers to find proof pointing to such within the Scriptures. Certainly within the Jewish Scriptures while there may be resuscitation to earthly life, as seen in the Elijah cycle with the great prophets, Elijah (1 Kgs 17:17-24) and Elisha, (2 Kgs 4:32-35, 2 Kgs 13:21)[1] there is nothing comparable to an immediate resurrection to glory, as claimed for Jesus. As we have already seen even in the inter-testamental period resurrection was not something having immediate effect, but was something which happened at the eschaton or end of time, nor was it to the earth, but rather to glory. Given such it is fair to conclude

---

[1] Elisha had asked for a double portion of Elijah's spirit and seemingly having witnessed Elijah ascend to the heavens in a winged chariot receives such. Therefore, having received double, while Elijah is the instrument through which God raises one from the dead, Elisha is the instrument through which two are raised from the dead. The last episode is largely unknown, but occurs when a man being buried in the grave of Elisha is restored to life upon touching the bones of the great prophet.

with Alan Richardson, 'The gospel story would hardly have contained a resurrection episode if it had been composed by learned rabbis out of Old Testament prophecies concerning a Messiah.'[2]

Given this cautious method of event construction, it is quite remarkable then that the early Christians, deeply imbued by their Jewish tradition, could construct something as radically new as the resurrection as we have it within the Christian Scriptures! Yet, as seen it became from very early on, the heart of their preaching. If it were not true then 'our faith is in vain' says Paul, 'and we are of all to be the most pitied.' (1 Cor 15:17-18) From the very first, in possibly his earliest epistle, Paul affirms it. (1 Thess 4:13-18) Further, when Paul makes his great statement of the resurrection in 1 Corinthians 15, he tells us he is passing on to them an already existing tradition preceding him (verses 1-7). It is also clearly evident in the Acts story, which purportedly speaks of the church's earliest preaching. (Acts 2:14-36, 3:12-26, 4:8-12, 5:29-32, 10:34-43)[3]

Let us now turn to more closely look at Jesus as presented in the gospels, and the understanding he brings to this question of resurrection. I say Jesus as presented in the gospels, rather than any real historical Jesus, as this is the only Jesus we have, with the Jesus presented by each gospel writer varying. The pursuit of the Jesus of history is an ongoing one, and although we can read through the gospels separating what is sometimes clearly editorial content placed on the lips of Jesus by the particular evangelist from what we believe to be the actual words of Jesus, this process is obviously one fraught with danger and difficulty. It is too easy clearly by circular argument, to find the Jesus we wish to find, doing so by judging those words and actions of Jesus which don't fit our favored schema, as being editorial pieces constructed by the evangelist. Of course Jesus scholars are acutely aware of this danger, taking great care to avoid it, but can never really escape it. One of the best known scholars in the modern search for the historical Jesus, John Dominic Crossan, when asked whether it was likely as an Irishman he would find a rebellious Jesus, commented frankly, 'probably'. Such honesty and recognition of the difficulties is not of

---

[2] Alan Richardson, An Introduction to the Theology of the New Testament S.C.M. London 1958
[3] We need of course to remember that this purported early preaching of course is colored by the author Luke's understanding, as he writes 55-80 years after what he describes. The wide range of dating reflects the current scholarly debate on the dating of this gospel.

course to negate the high degree of scholarship that goes into his, and other Jesus scholars' work, with Crossan himself going to extraordinary lengths to arrive at his conclusion, Jesus as the revolutionary.[4]

The only Jesus we can speak of with certainty is that as presented by Mark, Matthew, Luke or John (to limit ourselves to the canonical gospels), with the Jesus presented by each, as said, varying, sometimes significantly. Matthew presents a Jesus standing firm within his Jewish tradition, but opposed to the Judaism contemporaneous with him, which Matthew has him judge as being utterly corrupted. This conflict is more reflective of the opposition between the Matthean community and the Judaism of his time, than that of any actual conflict between Jesus and his tradition within his own time. Mark's Jesus is very much shaped by the 'Messianic secret' motif, whereby Jesus is presented as one continually admonishing those witnessing his great miracles or being recipients of his teaching, to 'keep mum' about it. This probably has to do with Mark's desire to present a Jesus marked by suffering and powerlessness, as corrective to 'power' understandings of the Messiah clearly growing within the church. One may compare Paul and his conflict with the Corinthian church in 1 Corinthians 12-13 on the same issue. Luke presents a Jesus who, although having an intense concern for the poor, represents no revolutionary threat to the Roman order. Luke, in both the gospel bearing his name and also in the Acts of the Apostles, has as his goal the presentation of an early Christian movement at home in the Roman Empire, thus giving us a Jesus at home in his own religio-cultural Jewish tradition. John's Jesus is presented as giving long profound sermons, very different from the pithy sayings and parabolic stories he presents in the synoptics. The Jesus of John's Gospel has a very elevated understanding of himself, identifying himself with the 'I am,' a circumlocution for the divine name, in such statements as, 'I am the door', 'I am the good shepherd', 'I am the way, the truth and the life,' among numerous others. Jesus is presented in John as one whose self-understanding is such that he believes the fulcrum of history revolves around him. He, and how one responds to him, is the determining factor, with the eschatological judgment already present in him. For John's Jesus eternal life

---

[4] John Dominic Crossan, The Historical Jesus: The Life of a Mediterranean Jewish Peasant, HarperCollins Publishers, United Kingdom, 1999, Jesus: A Revolutionary Biography, HarperCollins Canada 1994.

begins dependent in how one responds to him. This is what scholars call John's 'realized eschatology,' the end already being present in how one responds to Jesus. His preaching of himself, rather than the 'kingdom of God,' becomes core to this gospel. It is likely that if we were ever to meet John's Jesus, we would consider him an egotistical braggart, having highly inflated views concerning himself. What modern psychology would make of such a figure, believing himself to be divine, I will leave up to the reader. Of course these highly inflated saying on the lips of Jesus are thankfully not his, as an egotistical, dare I say delusional, braggart, but rather are the doxological expressions of those from the Johannine tradition. Understood as such, these claims to divinity can be seen in an entirely different, and indeed in an entirely positive light. They speak of the intensely profound influence Jesus had upon those who associated with him.

In conclusion then, I reiterate then that we must speak of the Markan, Matthean, Lukan or Johannine Jesus, with that being to limit ourselves to the canonical gospels. Having said all this as warning, we can also use this knowledge of the editorial goals of each of the gospels to assist us in seeking the actual Jesus of history. There are means in the discipline of biblical criticism to help us in this task, the main of which I will now briefly examine.

First, where independent traditions bear witness to Jesus' words or actions, it is more likely that they reflect something which Jesus said or did. That is more than just adding up the parallels as though they all count. We need to remember that Matthew and Luke both borrow directly from Mark, so just to say that three of the four gospels in common have Jesus saying or doing is not sufficient. Basically we look for multiple attestation from different sources, that which is Markan, that which is Matthean not borrowed from Mark and likewise that which is Lukan but not from Mark. Further there is that source above noted, called Q or Quelle (German, meaning source). Q does not exist as an extant document, but is created by scholars from material found in common in Matthew and Luke, but not having its genesis in Mark. Then, there is John, a very distinct tradition. Scholars used to pay it little regard in the search for the historical Jesus, but in more recent times are discovering layers of John, some of which may go back very early. We have just spoken of the canonical gospels. There were many others, but for the most part we can dismiss them as late creations, filled with ever more incredible stories to do with Jesus. The exception is the Gospel of Thomas, parts of which may pick up an authentic early tradition concerning Jesus. To Thomas we shall return.

Another important pointer to the genuineness or not of a gospel tradition concerning Jesus, is the criteria of embarrassment. If the account is embarrassing in that Jesus is presented as different to the norm of the tradition in which he stood, and/or from how he was already normally viewed in the infant church, then that account given in the embarrassing passage is likely to be true. Such a saying or event has such veracity that seemingly the tradition, though it has an interest in doing so, is unable to expunge it. Likewise, where Jesus is presented as saying something or doing something radically different to his norm.

Having established these parameters to guide us in our search, what do we find in our gospels to assist us in understanding Jesus' belief and practice of resurrection?

Of Jesus' practice we read that on three occasions he raises people from the dead; the daughter of Jairus, (Mark 5:21-24, 35-43 and pars) the son of the widow of Nain, (Luke 7:11-17) and in the best known instance, Lazarus. (John 11:1-44) We commence by looking at these accounts in that order.

The first instance commences with Jesus encountering a prostrate Jairus, a synagogue official with a daughter near death, who begs Jesus to accompany him. Following another story, the woman with 'the issue of blood' inserted between the two halves of the main story, a method the scholars call a 'Markan sandwich,' we are informed that the daughter has now died. Jesus chooses to ignore the report of her death, for he, unlike those around him, who now believed nothing further could be done, even by a healer as powerful as Jesus, instead believes that death itself need not be the end of the story, and that life, in the here and now, not just on the final day, could be restored. Leaving all except Peter, James and John, who seem to make up an inner triumvirate of those following him, Jesus enters the house of Jairus, whereupon he inquires as to the cause of all the 'weeping and wailing,' before informing everyone that the girl is not dead but only 'sleeping'. Of course Jesus' use of the word is not meant to deny her being actually dead but rather, used as a metaphor, shows that for him death, which clearly looks like sleep, is no more permanent than sleep itself. After putting everyone out except the parents and 'those who were with him,' he takes the girl's hand and speaking in Aramaic, preserved in the otherwise Greek text, tells her to get up, which she does to the amazement of all. In raising this girl Jesus acts in his own power, no reference being made to intercessory prayer to God for the divine to act. Jesus' power is seemingly sufficient to itself. Indeed, both in this story, and that other story it encompasses, the woman with the issue of blood, there is a touch of magic involved. A type of such power is seemingly associated with Jesus, drawn out of him automatically or magically by the woman's touch, while in the raising of Jairus' daughter the preservation of the Aramaic words by which Jesus invokes the resurrection, is as though the words themselves have a magical power as incantation. As noted no prayer is present in either account of the woman's healing, or of Jesus' raising of Jairus' daughter, prayer being a more sophisticated form of magic. Magic either works or it does not, and if it does not, then it has clearly failed, for it is automatic (literally meaning self-powered). Prayer, on the other hand, allows an out for failure, in that if its petition is not granted it can be said that the petitioner's plea was not in accord with the will of God. Magic as such is more primitive, and that probably reflects the primitive, or very early Christian tradition from which this story comes. Elsewhere Jesus uses actions or particular invocations which may be linked to magic. On one occasion he, after spitting on mud, rubs it into a blind man's eyes leading to a restoration of sight, (John 9:6) with this miracle then being developed by John in his usual style into an extensive teaching. (John 9:1-40) On another occasion, when a man born mute is brought before him, Jesus cures him by putting his fingers into his ears, spits and then touches the man's tongue before uttering a word, seemingly understood by the early church as having a type of magical power in that it was preserved, 'Ephphatha.' (Mark 7:32-35) In another case, a man born blind is brought before Jesus who on this occasion spits into his eyes and lays hands upon him, an action which brings only a partial cure, before re-trying laying hands upon him but this time looking upon the man 'intently,' something which brings a complete cure. (Mark 8:22-25)

Within the earliest Christian tradition there are a number of wonder-workers or magicians with power to even raise the dead. Although the Hebrew Scriptures strictly forbade all magic practices, (Lev 19:26;

Deut 18:10) and made 'witchcraft' a capital offense (Ex 22:18) there exists a long tradition of magical practice within the Jewish tradition. (1 Sam 28:7-25, 2 Kgs 21:6, Isa 3:18-23 [note the amulets], Ezek 13:17-23, and drawing of lots, 1 Sam 14:42, Jon 1:7) We find magic, as already seen, in the Christmas story with practitioners of magic, the Magi, offering their obeisance to the infant Jesus. (Matt 2: 1-12) The early followers of Jesus came into contact with magic, (Acts 8:9- 11; 13:6-12) while many ascribed Jesus followers miracle-working to magic. In the last of those episodes it appears that on the magician Elymas, who is hindering God's work, Paul works a greater magic, resulting in Elymas being struck blind. Many even considered the early Christians as a cult closely associated with magic. The word the Christians used of the 'medicine' (pharmakon) of the Eucharist they also used to disparage others practices as magic. Their magic was good, that of others, not. There was also a widespread use of Christian amulets and also holy oils for anointing.

After our excursus into magic, let us return to our resurrection stories. In the first, the raising of the daughter of Jairus, at its conclusion, we are told that Jesus gives the strange admonition not to tell anyone of what has just happened. It is totally unreal and incredible obviously to suspect that no one of the clearly large crowd would break the silence over this astonishing event! As such it surely is clear in reality that Jesus would have hardly had such an unrealistic expectation as to people's silence, this admonition to silence then on the part of those who have witnessed his great acts in actuality being a creation of Mark, known as the Messianic Secret. In reading Mark's gospel it is possible to find a number of these instances, and they carry over into Matthew and Luke in places where these gospels pick up Mark's words. There has been great debate as to Mark's intention in using the Messianic secret. Originally it was suggested in 1901 by William Wrede, the scholar who first noted this feature of the Marcan gospel, that the Messianic secret represented a denial of the Christian claim as to Jesus being the Messiah. This would seem strange, however, when it is so attached to what are clearly messianic events, and in no episode does Jesus deny he is the Messiah, but rather simply admonishes people to silence. If denial of Jesus being the Messiah was the intention of either Jesus himself or of Mark, then it would make no sense to associate it with such messianic actions and events, nor have Jesus never simply straight out deny that he is the Messiah. What is most likely the intention of the messianic secret is Mark's desire to move Jesus from being just a miracle worker operating by 'signs and wonders,' the usual literal translation of Jesus' 'miracles' in the synoptic gospels, to something deeper. Certainly Mark has a Jesus more marked by suffering than triumph. This, as I have already mentioned, serves as a corrective to the one-sided Christology of power, suffering acting to counter a one-sided emphasis on power spectacularly exhibited in such miracles as that we have been describing.

The placement of this Jairus story in each of the three synoptic gospels is part of a context, common to each of them, in which Jesus' power is clearly manifest over all things. Jesus heals a woman with a hemorrhage, stills the stormy waters, (Mark 4:35-41 and pars) exorcises the Gerasene victim of the demonic, (Mark 5:1-20 and pars) and now, this power culminates in him being able to even break open the gates of death itself. The Messianic secret seems to act as a filter through which to view these actions, seemingly with the goal of moving us beyond a place wherein we would see Jesus limited to being a magical miracle worker and nothing more. As incredible a miracle worker as Jesus is, something far deeper is being affirmed of him. The power over both water and death was something, which in both cases, belonged with the Divine.

The second resurrection performed by Jesus is that of raising the deceased son of the widow of Nain. This story is clearly midrash, built on a story from the Elijah cycle, wherein the greatest of Israel's prophets likewise raised a widow's son. (1 Kgs 17:8-24) Like nearly all Christian midrash it is meant to parallel, but also to trump the Jewish parallel. Thus so, where Elijah must implore 'the Lord' at least four times, while needing to cast himself upon the deceased son three times, Jesus does not even need to touch the deceased, a mere touching of the funeral bier seemingly sufficing, and rather than dramatically casting himself upon the deceased to implore the divine, Jesus simply quietly in his own power without any reference to God says, 'young man I say to you, arise.' (Luke 7:14) This mighty action understandably leads to the exclamation that, 'God has visited his people.' (Luke 7:16) This account being peculiar to Luke, thus coming later in the tradition, there is therefore no hint of magic, which may well have been associated with Elijah's throwing himself upon the corpse. Jesus, highly sovereign, has no need for any type of magical incantation, nor touching of the corpse to bring about the resurrection.

The third resurrection worked by Jesus is, as said, best known, the raising of Lazarus. This story, unlike that we have just viewed, is full of detail, that detail serving to make the story all the more spectacular. Within John's gospel there are seven – the number being sacred – miracles understood by John as signs (he uses the Greek word 'semeia' meaning sign of the miracles), commencing with the turning of the water into wine at the wedding in Cana of Galilee, and culminating with this final sign, the resurrection of Lazarus, which anticipates the resurrection to follow, that of Jesus himself. This Lazarus miracle is the culmination of that section of John's gospel, which scholars call 'the book of signs,' (John 1:19 – 12:50) within which John has these seven miraculous signs, interspersed with seven long passages of teaching or sermons given by Jesus. John uses this word, 'signs' to describe Jesus' miracles in order to preclude us from staying fascinated with the miracles themselves, instead being drawn to the deeper reality to which they point, hence the extensive teachings placed between each and built around them. The synoptic gospels on the other hand, use of the miracles the 'powers and wonders.' From this Lazarus story we move to the final section of John's Gospel, 'the book of glory,' (John 13:1 - 20:31) in which Jesus is glorified in his death, resurrection and ascension, each of those aspects, not just the resurrection, testifying to that glory, something to which I will return.

In his raising Lazarus Jesus is enacting that future resurrection expected of the final day but making it present. To Martha's belief, widespread at the time, that yes she believes Lazarus will rise on the last day, (John 11: 24) Jesus asserts that in him, the one who is 'the resurrection and the life,' and in whom belief guarantees life not death, that last day has already begun. He evidences that by his raising of Lazarus, not at the last day, something which Martha, echoing what clearly is contemporary Jewish orthodoxy, expects, but in the moment, right now at hand. As said John's Gospel has what is called a 'realized eschatology' in that the great salvation moment, along with judgment, occurs not at the culmination of history, the last day or eschaton, but rather is 'realized' in the Jesus moment, and here in the raising of Lazarus is a powerful witness to that. In Jesus' reply to Martha there does still however, seem to remain a future

Chapter Four: Jesus' understanding and practice

fuller resurrection yet to come. Thus he responds, 'whoever believes in me though they die yet shall they live, and whoever lives and believes in me shall never die.' (John 11: 25-26) Jesus is clearly speaking of death in two different manners. The first part seems to indicate that obviously, the believer like all others will die a physical death, as does, we would assume, Lazarus even after he has been raised, while the second part of the response appears to affirm that beyond that physical death, there is another dimension in which death understood as ultimate finality holds no more sway. In this story the metaphor 'sleep' is used for death. (John 11:11-13) So non-comprehending are the disciples of the metaphor, Jesus is forced to 'tell them plainly, Lazarus is dead.'

Again, Jesus in this account uses his own authority rather than that of God to carry out the resurrection, his looking to the heavens appearing to be so that the crowds will believe that God has sent him, rather than representing any real need for divine assistance. Such is confirmed in the words he says, 'Father I thank you that you have heard me, I know you always hear me, but I have said this on account of the people standing by, that they may believe that you sent me.' (John 11: 41-42) Any reference to God seems to be but a proper formality. There may be echoes in this in that it was believed that others had the power to raise from the dead, but were doing so, not in accord with the will of God. Those others seemingly act with the power of magic, or with the assistance of demonic powers, the two in the biblical understanding held to be essentially the same anyway. When we come to the actual moment of resurrection, without recourse to any sign of magic or to the Divine, but in his own power alone Jesus issues the command, 'Lazarus, come out.' (John 11:43) Jesus in this gospel understands himself as the one who gives judgment, the one in whom life or death is secured. He himself represents 'the resurrection and the life.' We find further evidence of such in John's Gospel where Jesus says, 'For as the Father raises the dead and gives them life, so also the son gives life to whom he will. The Father judges no one but has given all judgment to the son.' (John 5:21-22) Jesus in John's Gospel, has clearly already been elevated a way along a path to full divinity.

In those resurrection actions we have just examined Jesus has clearly broken with the accepted understanding of the resurrection, in that it would take place on the 'last day' of the eschaton. (John 11:24) Clearly the realized eschatology of John's Gospel colors the account of Lazarus' resurrection, where its immediate effect is contrasted with Martha's statement of belief that the resurrection will happen, but not until the last day. Yet the immediacy of resurrection enacted by Jesus is also evident, as we have seen in the other two resurrection accounts, in the synoptic gospels, without any need of a realized eschatology.

Each of these three resurrection accounts have taken the resurrection from something present on the 'final day,' to being something already happening, intimately linked to the action of Jesus. The three accounts make clear that it is Jesus himself, without need of recourse to God, who is the author of resurrection. In Jesus the sign of the final day, the day of resurrection sign of the Messianic reign, is already breaking in, so it is appropriate that those signs belonging to it, particularly the greatest, that of life destroying death, be made present in and through him. Yet Jesus' contact with resurrection is not exhausted by these three events.

Jesus is involved in an event on another occasion, which again provides evidence that the resurrection is not on the last day, but has already been made present in and by Jesus. In that episode, the Transfiguration, Jesus ascends a mountain with three of his followers, Peter, James and John, clearly representing an inner circle. (Mark 9:2-9 and pars) While there, they experience an incredible epiphany wherein Jesus appears transfigured before them in clothes brilliantly white, before they are joined by a resurrected Moses and Elijah. Peter, clearly awestruck, responds that he wishes to remain in such a place and construct three tents or booths for that purpose. This construction of booths indicates the Jewish harvest festival of Succot or Tabernacles, which had become associated with the gathering of all peoples at the time of the Messiah. That messianic time was the time of resurrection, so this event with its resurrected figures is meant to indicate that the messianic time had now already begun, it being made present in Jesus. That the epoch of resurrection had already begun caused confused questioning as to what this rising from the dead could mean (Mark 9:10) among the three witnesses, for it was clearly contrary from that which as we have seen was the accepted contemporary orthodoxy of the resurrection being associated with the 'last day.' The presence of Moses and Elijah both 'resurrected' is meant to indicate that this resurrection era has indeed commenced. Of course technically understood

Elijah was not resurrected, for in the tradition we are told he was taken directly to heaven and thus had never died. (2 Kgs 2:11)

Having surveyed Jesus' practice we shall now turn to his teaching, as distinct from his actions on the matter of resurrection. There are a number of instances in which we find Jesus speaking about the resurrection, but probably the core passage is that wherein he is in dispute with the Sadducees, who as we will remember did not believe in resurrection. (Mark 12:18-27 and pars) In this dispute Jesus holds firmly to the idea of resurrection meant as an individual's existence beyond the grave. Even if this represents a later catechetical elaboration by the church, as some have claimed, there seems to be a tradition behind the teaching picking up the genuine Jesus in his conflict on this matter with this conservative party. On the nature of the resurrection, we have already seen, how some understood it very literally as being raised back to the same plane with the same issues as one would have in human life, ruler and ruled, rich and poor for instance, but understanding that in resurrection life the roles would be reversed as a form of retributive justice. The Sadducees, as noted, would hardly have wanted such, a reversal of the economic and political order, for the current state of things suited them well.

In this account, those opposing the idea of resurrection, the Sadducees, can only understand it in such literalist manner, this being clear by the question they place before Jesus. They hold that in any supposed resurrected state, one would still carry out such earthly human things as marrying and would still be under the Mosaic Law. That Mosaic Law is crucial here for the discussion presupposes the Levirate law of marriage. By that law if a man died without leaving any sons to carry his name, it would be the brother's role to have intercourse with the deceased's wife, so as to produce the deceased's progeny. This represented the traditional manner of understanding progeny – that one would live on, not by being raised in resurrection, but by having one's name and lineage sustained through one's offspring. The Sadducees, thinking they are on to a good thing, sure to trap Jesus as representative of those believing in the resurrection, draw the story out to ridiculous lengths in their example, in an attempt to show the illogicality of resurrection. Thus they pose the question that if all seven brothers in turn have sought to ensure the original husband's progeny without success, given that she has been married to all seven brothers 'whose wife will she be in the resurrection?' Jesus' response is to assert that the age of resurrection is quantitatively different and there will be no need of marrying. Marriage was primarily about guaranteeing progeny, so to guarantee one's name lived on, that being symbolic of eternity. Obviously in Jesus' mind in the age of resurrection, with no dying, and therefore no need to replenish 'the stock,' in order to guarantee the continuity of one's name, there is therefore no need of marriage, nor of clearly sexual intercourse. The attitude held by the inquisitors, Luke judges to represent the distinction between 'the people of this age' and 'those considered worthy of taking part in the coming age and in the resurrection of the dead.' (Luke 20:34-35)

As to when the resurrection will be – immediate or at the eschaton – no clear view emerges in Jesus' teaching. In one important sense the fullness of resurrection is not experienced immediately as none of those raised by Jesus – Jairus' daughter, the son of the widow of Nain and Lazarus – are raised to immortality, with each, it must be assumed, having to expire physically at some future stage, the portal of physical death being after-all something through which even Jesus will need to pass. The fullness of the resurrection is therefore not exhausted in the resurrection acts carried out by Jesus, these being more anticipatory than final. Elijah and Enoch remain the only two from within the tradition who do not pass through death's otherwise universal portal. There is some speculation in the Christian Scriptures as to what will happen to those alive at the time of the parousia, the coming again of the Christ, it being surmised by Paul that those believers alive at the time of that event, would likewise be taken to heaven without experiencing death. (1 Thess 4:17)

Jesus it seems holds to the contemporary orthodox view that the resurrection is something which in its fullness, is future, associated with the 'last day.' His resurrection actions, as miraculous as they are, need to be, understood in light of such, as anticipatory signs, for as fantastic as they are, they do not exhaust the full miracle of resurrection, for they after-all are resurrections not to eternity, but to temporality, not to the heavens with full intimacy with the Divine, but to the earth.

Chapter Four: Jesus' understanding and practice

There is however, one occasion when it appears that Jesus, who always gives resurrection in his own power rather than with reference to the Divine, makes the resurrection he gives something absolute and final, without reference to the eschaton or 'final day.' Jesus, in his dying breath, does so when he promises the rebel hanging on the cross along with him instant translation into paradise. (Luke 23:40-43)[5] This well-known instance is not however well attested, with both Mark and Matthew indicating that both of those crucified beside Jesus cursed him. Even here this man necessarily will need to still pass through, given his circumstances, a very painful portal of death.

Jesus clearly links his own resurrection with the reign of God, which he understands as commencing in it. This is clearly the case in John's Gospel with its realized eschatology, but is also present in the synoptic gospels. The strongest synoptic evidence lies, as noted, in the account of the Transfiguration. In this episode we have seen how Jesus' resurrection is understood as an anticipatory sign of the new resurrected life, of all things extending to the cosmos itself. Thus, following the actual Transfiguration as they descend the mountain, Jesus admonishes James and John concerning this event, 'not to tell anyone until the son of man has risen from the dead' at the commencement of the messianic age. (Mark 9:9, Matt 17:9) As we have found, the Transfiguration is a vision of that Messianic age, a vision of the reign of God, where both the Law (Moses), and the prophets (Elijah), are present, and in this episode that vision is inextricably linked with Jesus' resurrection.

That strong connection between Jesus' resurrection and the eschaton is seen on another occasion. While in Jerusalem, one of the disciples comments on the magnificence of the temple to which Jesus replies that it will be torn down 'stone upon stone,' (Mark 13:1-2 and pars) this serving as the basis of a charge brought against him before the Sanhedrin during his trial, where it was alleged that he also said that after destroying the

---

[5] This man is usually called 'a thief.' In reality dying thus, crucified, a punishment reserved almost exclusively for rebels, it is more likely the thieving he was carrying out was as a rebel against the empire. Jesus is linked with such a rebel figure, Barabbas (John 18: 40) with whom he is drawn in opposition. This opposing is late in the tradition, probably representing an attempt to dissociate Jesus from his rebel roots. Barabbas literally meaning in Hebrew, 'son of the father,' is clearly a created figure, as is the whole episode in which he appears, as a foil to Jesus who is understood as 'son of the Father' (ie God).

temple, 'in three days I will build another not made with human hands.' (Mark 14:58 and pars) In that statement Jesus' resurrection is linked with a greater eschatological temple of the messianic age, in which true union with the divine and all things, such role being proper to the temple, will be found. In like manner at his trial Jesus seems to claim that God's reign will commence 'when you see the son of man coming on the clouds with great power and glory.' (Mark 14:62) Again, from the same section of Mark's Gospel we have Jesus once more link events to do with him to the eschatological reign of God, saying of eating the bread and drinking the cup at the Last Supper, 'truly I say to you, I shall not drink again of the fruit of the vine until that day I drink it new in the kingdom of God.' (Mark 14:25) Clearly in Jesus the eschaton has commenced, and clearly the central sign of that eschaton is resurrection. When Jesus is resurrected, or resurrects himself, and we will look later at that changing understanding in the scriptural account, resurrects others, or in the case of the Transfiguration, acts as the cause of resurrection appearances, clearly he is understood as being core to the eschaton, which commences in him, being anticipated by these resurrection experiences.

Yet there is an ambiguity about those resurrections Jesus enacts or announces. In each of those three central cases we have discussed – the daughter of Jairus, the widow's son, and Lazarus – clearly the resurrections, as miraculous as they are, are not final and complete, yet elsewhere, as they are in his own resurrection, and that which he announces to the thief, completion is already present. In those former cases resurrection is a type of resuscitation back to the earth, still in corporeal, therefore mortal form, whereas in the latter two instances resurrection is to heaven in a non- corporeal and therefore immortal form. As we shall see later the Evangelists will take Jesus out of that second category and place him in a halfway place between the two, resurrection back to the earth in corporeal form, but in that form having no need to die, for he will, like Elijah, be taken to the heavens directly.

On occasions Jesus emphasizes his resurrection as being the crucial event in which the eschaton or final reality of God's reign is breaking into history, with the effects of that being immediately available to believers, whereas at other times he seems to understand judgment, and therefore a believer's resurrection life, as being future, taking place at the eschaton, associated with his return or parousia. We find the latter in the apocalyptic passages found in each of the synoptic gospels, where the eschaton with Jesus' parousia, rather than his resurrection, being clearly central. On three successive illustrations Jesus speaks of how with two men in a field, two women grinding grain and two in bed, on each occasion one will be raptured away to salvation while the other will be left.(Matt 24:40-44, Luke 17:34-37) Again, the eschaton is central in the parable following, which tells of how one needs to be prepared for the master who may come at any time. (Matt 24:45-51 and pars) In like manner the final judgment takes center stage in the parable of the weeds, (Matt 13:24-30, 36-43) as well as in the parable of the sheep and the goats. (Matt 25:31-46) In these apocalyptic passages, Jesus speaks of himself as the son of man coming, 'on clouds with great power and glory, when he will send out the angels, and gather his elect from the four winds, from the ends of earth, from the ends of heaven.' (Mark 13:26-27 and pars) These apocalyptic passages found in the synoptic gospels sound very similar to the genre commonly found in Jewish writing of the time, the role of the Messiah having much in common with contemporary Jewish expectations. I therefore, don't hold much credence in them, which is not the same as saying, I do not believe that Jesus had an apocalyptic side to his preaching. Because the passages are so traditional however, they lack authenticity as being from the lips of Jesus, instead representing part of the developing tradition.

That apocalyptic role, however, is present in another context, that of Jesus before the Sanhedrin. There, in response to the question, 'are you the Christ (Messiah) son of the Blessed (God)?' Jesus responds, 'I am, and you will see the Son of man seated at the right hand of power, and coming with the clouds of heaven.' (Mark 14:62) It is this statement which finally determines Jesus' destiny. Though this statement is only present in Mark and Matthew, and not in Luke, in this context it has a sound of authenticity about it. In such statements it would appear that Jesus understands himself as having a central apocalyptic role on the final day when judgment shall be issued.

Yet, at the heart also of the charges made against Jesus, is that he was charged to have said, 'I will destroy this temple that is made with human hands, and in three days I will build another, not made with hands.' (Mark 14:58 and pars). If this charge is correct, and Mark thinks it is not, (Mark

14:59) Jesus is apparently saying that the great eschatological temple associated with the Messianic era has commenced in him, with the three days having clear reference to his resurrection. The great day of judgment, the eschatological 'final day,' is about to begin in his approaching death and subsequent resurrection and return. John, contrary to Mark, confirms that indeed Jesus did make this statement, (John 2:19-21) though strangely while John is the only gospel to have Jesus say these words, they form no part of the charges brought against him in that gospel. This claim by John may have little credibility, however, given that he has moved the whole temple cleansing episode from where in reality it surely must lie, at the culmination of Jesus' ministry, to the beginning of his gospel. This three days concerning the temple destruction and rebuilding having reference to Jesus' resurrection is something which interestingly Jesus' opponents seem to understand before those who are his followers. (Matt 27:63)

Ambiguously both ideas of immediate judgment, dependent on one's response to Jesus in the eschatological moment made present, and the idea that judgment for all comes on the 'last day,' sit together in John's Gospel. (John 5:19-30) There Jesus proclaims, 'for the hour is coming, and now is, when the dead will hear the voice of the Son of God and those who hear will live. For as the Father has life in himself, so he has granted the son also to have life in himself, and has given authority to execute judgment, because he is the son of man. Do not marvel at this; for the hour is coming when all who are in the tombs will hear his voice and come forth, those who have done good to the resurrection of life, and those who have done evil, to the resurrection of judgment.' (John 5: 25-29) In the initial part of this statement it seems only those who rise to live hear Jesus' voice and do so in the present, whereas in the latter part all will hear his voice, being raised, either to life or condemnation, but at the future eschaton. In such a passage we see at work the fullness of Johannine theology with its 'realized eschatology,' that theological view clearly informing the first part of this discourse, where for the believer, eternal life begins in the now of Jesus' presence and one's reception of him. Despite this, in the latter part of the discourse clearly the fullness of the eschaton and the judgment it brings, though centered on Jesus, is not yet fully realized, such only occuring at the eschaton. There still remains a future climax. Another major theme in John's theology, the high Christology concerning Jesus is, however, clearly seen throughout the discourse. Jesus himself is the author of life, given power to execute judgment. We find Jesus speaking of himself, almost as proxy of God, being the judge, with that judgment happening in the very present, dependent on how one hears and responds to Jesus' word. (John 5:19-24)

Again, despite the realized eschatology of this gospel, Jesus speaks three times in one chapter with identical words placing the resurrection at the eschaton: 'and I will raise them up on the last day.' (John 6:40,44,54) In these statements the high Christology of John is again present, judgment being centered on Jesus. Indeed, so high is John's Christology one's resurrection is entirely dependent on how they respond to Jesus. 'Those who reject me and do not receive my sayings has a judge; the word that I have spoken will be their judge on the last day.' (John 12:48) To Thomas' query as to how to find the way to salvation Jesus responds, 'I am the way, the truth and the life; no one comes to the Father, but by me.' (John 14:6) So linked is eternal life with Jesus, he is the one who prepares its abode, 'In my father's house there are many rooms; if it were not so would I have told you that I will go to prepare a place for you? And when I go and prepare a place for you, I will come again and take you to myself, that where I am you may be also.' (John 14:2-3) Here judgment is centered totally in Jesus, through whom access to eternal life is won, and though there is an aspect of 'return,' (John 14:3) that return rather than being at some eschatological judgment, appears immediate. Clearly, though Jesus is always central to resurrection, there is a tension between resurrection, placed on the future eschaton linked to the parousia, or being something already commenced, made present, in the Jesus event, particularly in his resurrection.

Jesus seemingly believes in a twofold resurrection, the righteous to reward and the unrighteous to punishment. This twofold resurrection, either to glory or judgment, is, however, strongly linked to the eschaton, where such judgement takes place, the parable of the sheep and the goats serving as the best known testimony. (Matt 25: 31-46) The twofold resurrection is seen also in the parable of the weeds. (Matt 13:24-30, 36-43) Here the eschatological emphasis is particularly strong, for when the servants in the story ask the master as to whether they should now go out into the field to pluck out and separate the weeds, they are told not to do so but rather let the crop and the weeds grow together until harvest when at that time they will be separated, the weeds to be burned, the produce to be kept. Judgment here is in a purely a future eschatological dimension, the parable after-all calling one away from judging in the here and now. In the same chapter of Matthew's gospel, the parable of the net, we have another like parable with the emphasis on separation in judgment being at the eschaton. (Matthew 13:47-50) In this parable the net operates as a kind of catch all, representing the proclamation delivered by Jesus, which catches both the good and bad 'fish,' sieving them by their response to the word. Here it is made obvious that this is an eschatological judgment for we are explicitly told, 'so it will be at the close of the age. The angels will come out and separate the evil from the righteous, and throw them into the furnace of fire, where people will weep and gnash their teeth.' These last few words are used a number of times in the telling of such stories, clearly representing a traditional formula. That almost certainly shows that these type of parables represent in their final form, something more traditional, reflecting the contemporary Jewish belief in the final resurrection rather than any actual words of Jesus. In their original forms the parables appear to have been ethical injunctions but are then later developed around the idea of eschatological judgment, this done in a traditional manner.

The twofold resurrection is also present in the parable of the good and the bad servant, (Matt 24:45-51, Luke 12:41-46) where the faithful servant, ready for their master's coming, is rewarded by resurrection to life, while his ill-prepared colleague will suffer punishment. Still, the idea of such judgment being connected to one's eternal destiny seems to be a later development of this story, which initially again seems originally limited to an ethical call to be ready in service.

Jesus not only speaks of a twofold resurrection to reward, but also to punishment. This is most vividly picked up in an image, full of hyperbole, when he says, 'Whoever causes one of these little ones who believe in me to sin, it would be better for them if a great millstone were hung around their neck and they were thrown into the sea. And if your hand causes you to sin, cut it off; it is better for you to enter life maimed than with two hands to go to hell, to the unquenchable fire... where the worm does not die and the fire is never quenched.' (Mark 9: 42-48) As we have seen, this is representative of literal understandings of a physical resurrection from within the tradition. The terrible scourge of clerical paedophilia makes this saying all too poignant in the modern context.

In conclusion, we may say Jesus seems to assert both a future and present transformed reality in light of the reign of God. The reign is experienced for the believer in the current moment, but will not be fully experienced, even in John's Gospel with its realized eschatology, until one passes into the domain of eternal life after death, where judgment for both the virtuous and the evil takes place as a finality at the eschaton. The focus of that traditional Jewish eschatological judgment is, however, radically changed, now centered on how one responds to Jesus as Messiah.

Jesus has an understanding of the resurrection clearly built around ethics, with judgment, either to glory or to punishment, being determined by how a person has lived. We find such clearly in the episode when asked by a 'wealthy man' as to what he must do in order to inherit eternal life. (Mark 10:17-22 and pars) On hearing Jesus' response, that he must keep the commandments; the Torah, the man replies that he has kept to all the strictures of the Law. Jesus then commands him to sell all he has and give the proceeds to the poor. As we no doubt know, the man cannot do so, and goes 'away sorrowful for he had great possessions.' In such we see Jesus' understanding of eternal life as being clearly something intimately linked to ethical living, ethics initially having to do with the keeping to the Torah, but then driving deeper to that which lay behind the Law, an equitable distribution of wealth, which would preclude any falling back into the slavery represented by this poverty, from which in Egypt, they had escaped long before. This concern for justice so all may live in freedom and dignity lies at the heart of the Torah, forming the basis for so many of its proscriptions. Jesus is making eternal life the reward for something far deeper than mere account keeping of how one has fulfilled the strictures of the Law. After the rich man leaves, unable to meet the ethical challenge, Jesus speaks to his close circle charging, those who give up the things of wealth in this world, 'for my sake and the gospel' will immediately receive recompense of the same things given up 'in this age' but also 'eternal life in the age to come.' (Mark 10:30, Luke 18:30 cf Matthew 19:29) Both present and future dimensions are again present. As a precaution against an early form of 'prosperity gospel' a later insertion, I contend, as to receiving also 'increased persecution' is inserted.

On another occasion, Jesus on likewise being asked by a 'young lawyer,' as to what he need do to receive eternal life, (Luke 10:25) responds with a question of his own concerning what is contained in the Torah. The young man responds by quoting that prayer still daily recited by pious Jews, the Shema, 'You shall love the Lord with all your heart, soul, strength and mind' (Deut 6:6) joining that with another command, to love one's neighbor as oneself. (Lev 19:18) The man then, in what Luke in editorial comment charges as being the man's attempt to justify himself, asks 'who is my neighbor?' The response of Jesus is to tell the story of 'the good Samaritan.' (Luke 10:30-37) The question of what a person must do to receive eternal life, is met with a story from Jesus, all about ethical just living, of breaking down boundaries and barriers between people.

Jesus' emphasis on the ethical demand concerning eternal life is again seen when he states that not even a careless word should be said lest it imperils one's salvation. (Matt 12:35-37) Such careless words break the communal fabric, with that clearly understood by Jesus, as imperiling one's reception of eternal life.

Again in those stories we previously examined, – the parables of the weeds and the net, along with the sheep and goats – eschatological judgment is rooted absolutely in the ethical dimension. How one lives is determinative of how one will be judged in the resurrection.

Centered on ethics, the eschatological resurrection leads to a great reversal of fortune from that now experienced. Luke in particular has a concern for this reversal of fortunes, often having in his gospel, as in the Magnificat, the poor being lifted up, while the high and mighty are cast down. (Luke 1:39-55) Such understanding drew strongly upon ideas current, indeed ideas which as seen, were largely responsible for the genesis of the idea of resurrection, within Judaism, the reversal of fortune which the resurrection brings as a type of divine retributive justice.

This essential connection between resurrection to eternal life and one's ethical living, is again picked up in another story Luke gives, that of Lazarus and so-called Dives. (Luke 16:19-31) This parable strongly emphasizes that reward and punishment will be not only in a time following death, but also in a different geographical domain, a place to which one would be sent, either a place of punishment or one of reward based on one's deeds. This parable sounds very different to Jesus' norm, mainly in both the detail and imagery it contains. It would seem to be a traditional story of the time which Luke, and the story is found only in Luke, has used to make the point of one's earthly duty of just and compassionate caring. (Luke 16:25) Jesus perhaps originally told a story of Lazarus and the poor man at his gate to make an ethical point, charging that such inequality and lack of concern for the poor is clearly is contrary to the Torah. Only later did a classical type of apocalyptic judgment motif get attached to it, that apocalyptic story being drawn from a very traditional pool of such stories.

Luke's strong concern for the eschatological reversal of all things is evident once more in his parable of the banquet, given while he himself is at table. (Luke 14:1-14) Table fellowship was, and still is, crucially important throughout the Middle East, strongly associated with both honor and with shame. In order to both gain honor and avoid shame, great care was taken in just who one invited to their table, and to which invitations one accepted to other tables. On arrival at a 'worthy' table, again careful calculation was made as to just how high one could sit precisely to avoid what happens in this story given by Jesus, being asked to vacate your seat for one more important who arrives late, as inevitably 'important' people do, so as to be noticed. As an aside to the oft-asked question as to whether Jesus has humor, this story affirms he indeed had a deep wry type of humor. Such table feast, especially when it is a wedding feast, as in this parable, is also representative of the messianic feast. (Isaiah 25:6) Thus, when Jesus tells this story, he is speaking of the messianic feast in which all those things normally associated with 'table,' will be overturned or reversed. The feast of the resurrected is one of radical open commensality. To this feast will be invited all who are regarded as 'sinners,' – 'the poor, the maimed, the lame, the blind.' In conclusion, Jesus speaks of one's reward for inviting such people being 'at the resurrection of the just.' (Luke 14:14) In this case there seems to be no general resurrection, with some going to judgment, but merely a raising of those 'bound for glory.' It may be implied however, that those already invited back to the tables of those they considered worthy, have already received their reward, and at the eschaton receive their 'just desserts.' Judgment may perhaps be implied, though only exclusion, rather than active punishment.

Where for Jesus is the place of resurrection? This is generally less specifically detailed, but the reward is mostly seen to be a pleasant heavenly abode called paradise. (Luke 23:43, 2 Cor 12:3, Rev 2:7) The origin of that place was Persia, its meaning etymologically being a nobleman's park or garden. We learn from the Matthean Lord's Prayer that God dwells in heaven, (Matt 6:9) and so to dwell with God was to dwell there. Thus, the lives of the believers will culminate in an eternal existence in such place with God (Rom 6:4-5, 1 Cor 2:9, Col 3:1, 1 John 3:2) The opposite of paradise was Gehenna, this, as we observed, originally referred to the valley of Hinnom, near Jerusalem, the place where child sacrifice was once offered to the god Moloch, by two kings, Ahaz (2 Chron 28:3) and Manasseh. (2 Chron 33:6)

Before turning from Jesus teachings and actions concerning resurrection, we need to remember that the idea of resurrection is not at the heart of Jesus' teaching, though he does assert it, as we have seen, strongly against the Sadducee non-belief. The heart of his teaching is clearly what he calls the kingdom of God. This is the 'shalom,' the holistic creation of right relationships between people, the creation/cosmos, and with God. In short, it is about justice, peace, sustainability, reconciliation and the harmonious relationship of all things. That more constant theme is picked up specifically in the beatitudes, (Matt 5:1-12) but more generally right through his parables and preaching on the kingdom of God/Heaven. Individual resurrection to another domain appears rather incongruous with Jesus' view of the totality of the renewal of all things, within this realm. Resurrection only makes sense when understood in the light of this reign of God as anticipatory sign. As such, resurrection comes as reward to those who have committed themselves to the path of the reign of God. So associated in popular thought has the gospel of Jesus become with the idea of some type of individual survival after death, often understood to be in some disembodied spiritual form, the understanding that the reign of God lay at the heart of his teaching, comes as great shock to many. A cursory reading of the synoptic gospels will confirm the centrality of the reign of God in Jesus' teaching, and such should be expected of one originally identified with being the Jewish Messiah.[6]

---

[6] 'We must finally break away from the idea that the gospel deals with the salvation of an individual's soul.' Dietrich Bonhoeffer, Gesammelte Schriften, 4:202

Chapter Four: Jesus' understanding and practice

What then can we conclude concerning Jesus' understanding and practice of resurrection? It seems no consistent pattern emerges. Sometimes there is a twofold resurrection, the righteous to glory, and the evil to judgment and punishment, while on other occasions it seems only the righteous are raised. There is, however, a preference for a twofold resurrection, though it is difficult to tell just how much Jesus' teachings as we have them, are being influenced by traditional understandings of resurrection and judgment contemporary with him, or are reflections of an early church influenced by traditional understandings. Certainly given the idea of resurrection arose because of the suffering of the righteous at the hands of the unjust oppressor, the idea of retributive justice plays an important role. The obvious oppressors at the time of Jesus were the Roman colonizers, and clearly part of popular views concerning resurrection would be along the lines that 'they will get theirs.' Retributive justice is understandably a powerful influence in shaping the views of the oppressed. We may prefer a Jesus not shaped by such populist base instincts, and therefore prefer to argue that the idea of judgment and punishment is something not associated with him. This, however, may well be another way of domesticating Jesus, who after all was shaped by a fiercely burning desire for the justice represented by the reign of God. Such zeal is clearly picked up in Jesus saying, 'I came to cast fire upon the earth; and would that were already kindled.' (Luke 12:49)[7] In any case we can be sure that ethics was central to resurrection for Jesus, indeed the determining factor. Again, this makes sense when we remember the ethical quandary which served as the basis for resurrection belief.

Again, with the question of whether Jesus understood the resurrection as immediate or eschatological, similarly no consistency emerges. Certainly when Jesus enacts resurrection on the three occasions he does, the effects are immediate rather than 'on the last day,' but these events are probably best understood as resuscitations as the recipient will still die at a future

---

[7] We may not like to think of Jesus being an apocalyptic figure, yet it is clear that apocalyptic understandings featured in Jesus' recorded teachings. We know that John the Baptist deeply influenced Jesus, with there being little doubt as to the apocalyptic lying at the heart of his preaching, and that Jesus' earliest followers embraced the apocalyptic, so ipso facto it is highly likely that Jesus, however much we may dislike it, held a strong strain of the apocalyptic. John Dominic Crossan calls it an ethical apocalyptic, or ethical eschatology, in that it called him and his followers to ethical living in the here and now.

point. The resuscitation events as such are best understood as anticipatory signs of the eschatological reality. If we limit 'resurrection' to those times where Jesus speaks of it in the sense of an event which following it, death shall no longer hold any sway, he tends to emphasize resurrection in the traditional eschatological manner.

Let us now turn to examine the resurrection of Jesus himself.

Chapter Five

Jesus' Resurrection - Gospel truth?

What was the nature of the Jesus' own resurrection as understood by the writers of the accounts we have of it? This questioning concerning the nature of Jesus' resurrection, and whether it is essential to believe in one particular form, will serve as the central issue around which I will shape this discussion. I shall conclude that the view we take as Christian orthodoxy, the physical resurrection of a corporeal body to the earth, before subsequent ascension to heaven, is not the only possible understanding, but indeed represents an understanding subsequent to others, which stood before it, among the earliest of the Christian believers.

To commence, it is good to dismiss what I can only regard to be the silly, though often spoken, ideas claiming that Jesus was only swooning in the tomb, not really dead when taken down from the cross, subsequently recovering from his wounds, so that it appeared that he had risen from the dead. I am sure most of us have heard this type of reasoning if one deigns to call it that. Jesus, not really dead when taken from the cross, in the cool of the tomb managed to revive, and having revived, walked from the tomb, after by himself rolling aside the 'heavy stone.' This all assumes that the Romans were so inept so as not to be able to carry out a crucifixion, despite their vast experience with this form of execution, which they exercised upon many thousands of insurrectionists and other 'criminals.' It further assumes that Jesus, despite a severe lashing, so severe that it probably of itself almost killed him, hanging asphyxiating in absolute agony, for that is the way the Romans designed this instrument of torture and social correction to kill, then having a spear run through his side, was not dead! The reality of course was that this J.C. was as dead as that other J.C. (Julius Caesar) after he likewise had been 'run through.' To give the Romans credit, they knew how to kill! It was a 'dark art' in which they were well practiced, having learned it very well. Crucifixion, they used frequently to kill in a particular gruesome and torturous manner.

Further, we learn from all the accounts that the resurrected Jesus had a transformed body. If his 'resurrected' body had been in actual brutal continuity with the crucified body, then it would have been very easy for those who witnessed him to indeed know it was him. His being three-quarters dead, his body draped with blood, and the brutal seeping lashes upon his back, his limping on pierced feet, would have been enough for his close friends to immediately know that it was him. Yet, they did not. The resurrected body, while being that of Jesus and still physical, seemingly was transformed in some manner, to make such easy identification not possible. This is definitely not a case of a heavily tortured person, still alive despite his torturers' understanding of them as being dead!

It is also claimed that Jesus' resurrection appearances are the result of some sort of widespread delusional psychosis. I say widespread because there are many such appearances, with a substantial number of people subject to them. It is far too convenient to say that such appearances represent psychological projections, arising out of either distress or disappointment, over their loss of Jesus and therefore their psychologically compensating for the failure of his mission, to which they had dedicated themselves. Some go as far as to speak even of an organized fraud. This is all quite possible with a small number of people but not, I hold, with large numbers on a variety of occasions. Michael Goulder, once an Anglican priest and now atheist, speaks of 'cognitive dissonance theory' to explain the appearances to both Peter and Paul, claiming that those appearances were means to resolve guilt felt by both of them; Peter for his denial of Jesus in his hour of need, and Paul for his earlier opposition to the Jesus movement. Further, he charges, both Peter and Paul are subject also to other visions, Peter at the Transfiguration and with the visit of Cornelius, (Acts 10:9-13) while Paul openly speaks of his 'excess of revelations.' (2 Cor 12:7) Goulder quotes the psychoanalyst Carl Jung: 'fanaticism is only found in individuals who are compensating secret doubts. The incident on the way to Damascus marks the moment when the unconscious complex of Christianity broke through into consciousness. Unable to conceive of himself as a Christian, on account of his resistance to Christ, he became blind and only could regain his sight through complete submission to Christianity.'[1] As for the large numbers spoken of as witnessing the risen Christ, 500 being mentioned at one stage by Paul, (1 Cor 15:6) Goulder charges,

---

[1] C G Jung, Contributions to Analytical Psychology, E.T.; New York 1945: 257 quoted p.60

they were deliberately or unconsciously lying, as having followed Jesus during his lifetime, this was a means of investing that choice with meaning, rather than suffering the anguish of it being understood as a lost cause. What Goulder says is interesting, in that true, there was no need originally for a physical resurrection to give rise to the belief that Jesus in some way had transcended the grave. The earliest resurrection experiences to Peter, Paul and others he notes, were all experiential visions, with no physicality involved. The increasing emphasis on the physicality of the resurrection, Goulder believes, was the prime means of refuting the charge that it was only delusional. This physicality of resurrection is first hinted in Mark's Gospel, and to the obvious question which would have been posed at this time, as to why we have not previously heard about this style of resurrection, he concludes, is given by Mark informing us, 'the women were afraid and said nothing' concerning it. (Mark 16:8)

    I see several faults with this without denying the power of the mind to consciously or otherwise project, deep desires and make compensation for guilt and doubt. First, while it may have been possible for 'individuals' as Jung notes, to be compensating 'secret doubts' and thus so Goulder speaks of both Peter and Paul, it would seem to me impossible for such large numbers, 500 on one occasion, to simultaneously hold such a vision. Crowds may be mesmerized by a speaker and whipped into a fanatical frenzy, and the Nuremberg rallies come to mind, but even on such an occasion there is no experience to compare to that which may be described as resurrection. Further, when the cost of bearing witness to Christ became such, that it could cost one one's life, it is unlikely that the early Christians would have held onto belief in the resurrection, if delusional or fraudulent. Even if held unconscious in nature, it would have been likely in many of the numerous cases, to resolve itself in face of the number of cruel methods Rome devised to deal with this cult of Christianity. Again, as earlier noted, there were a number of other possible responses to Jesus' failure, than that of wish-fulfillment; anger and resignation being two which come to mind. We can hardly assume that wish-fulfillment concerning Jesus, led all his followers into delusion, particular in style, namely that he had risen from the dead.

    Having dealt with such, let us turn to the resurrection appearances of Christ as given in the Christian Scriptures. On so turning to these stories found in our four canonical gospels, to which we will limit ourselves, and in Paul's understanding given in his various epistles, we immediately find there is very little in common, something entirely contrary to the crucifixion stories, which present a high level of consistency. It would seem that the crucifixion stories were extant, either as a fairly set oral or maybe written tradition before any of the gospels were written, many scholars believing them to be the earliest piece of Christian literature. The resurrection stories, on the other hand, due to their inconsistency cannot claim such early status, for apparently the writers in each tradition have flexibility to create their varying accounts, a flexibility they clearly didn't have with a strongly set crucifixion tradition. Indeed of all the episodes of Jesus' life, except for his clearly mythological birth, the greatest diversity in the accounts is found in the resurrection accounts.

Let us first turn to the earliest resurrection tradition. It may surprise many to find us not turning first to one of the gospels, but rather to the writings of Paul. Paul was executed in Rome in the mid-sixties of the first century, meaning all his writings pre-date our first gospel, that of Mark, written around 70CE.

Paul never accompanied Jesus, in all likelihood never meeting him during his earthly life. If he had done so, it would have been in a spirit of enmity, for Paul during the period of Jesus' ministry, was still Saul, an orthodox Jew and self-described enemy of this heterodox Jesus movement. His connection with, and understanding of Jesus, was purely with the post- resurrected Christ, following his conversion thrice described in the book of Acts, chapters 9, 22, 26. We need again to remind ourselves that Paul in all his extensive writings, says virtually nothing of the earthly Jesus. Paul either knows little of his ministry, or attaches no importance to it, even stating that he has no interest in 'Christ from a human point of view.' (2 Cor 5:16) This is particularly enlightening when we remember just how often Paul was pushing certain moral and ethical positions. Yet, despite this constant ethical concern, he never once argues in a manner which says my way is right, for did not Jesus himself teach the same as I am now teaching? For Paul Jesus is always the already resurrected Christ who manifests himself to him as revelation. Paul's teachings are those based, not on any memories of an earthly Jesus, but on what he perceives and understands, as the resurrected Christ revealing himself to him.

Now let us turn to the manner in which Paul believes the resurrection took place, for in so doing we are in for surprises, perhaps even shock. This is because our understanding of the resurrection is so shaped by what became later orthodoxy, it is hard, almost impossible, for us to escape that understanding. In reading Paul's accounts our eyes are so blinkered or even blinded by later interpretations, we may 'look but not see.' The common view with which we have become familiar, to such depth, that we implicitly believe it to be the only view, understands Jesus having a physical or corporeal resurrection back to the world. Such understanding however, finds no place in Paul's writings. Rather, Paul has a spiritual resurrection, though no less real, not to the earth, but rather directly to God. Why do I say no less real? I do so because clearly Paul believes that the faith lives or falls by the reality of the resurrection. 'If there is no resurrection of the dead, Christ has not been raised, then our preaching is in vain, and your faith is in vain…if for this life only we have hoped in Christ, we are of all most to be pitied.' (1 Cor 15:13-20) For Paul, the resurrection is absolutely real, but not in the manner it is commonly understood by us. To the oft-made fundamentalist claim that the Christian faith stands or falls by the physicality of the resurrection, Paul would have answered emphatically, 'no'.

The earliest account of the resurrection from Paul is found in 1 Thessalonians, possibly the earliest of his letters, written around 51C.E. In it he is keen to clarify the nature of the resurrection, probably in response to a question that community had asked him. In 1 Thessalonians 4:13-17 we read of the resurrection, that it will take place for all, at the end of time, something clearly soon expected. At that time of the parousia (the return of Christ), both the living and the dead would be caught up together… in the clouds to meet the Lord in the air.' (1 Thess 4:17) Given his concern with the physicality of those still bodily living, it seems that Paul at this early stage in his thought, probably conceived of the resurrection as being somehow corporeal for both the living and those who had deceased. As found earlier, such a crudely physical view would not be unique in Israel, for some rabbinic scholars thus understood it. This need not be understood overly literally however, as Paul has a multivalent understanding of 'soma' or body, he using that word to not only to refer to the terrestial body, be it that of a human, animal, bird or fish, but also to celestial bodies. (1

Cor 15:39-40) Further, these ascending bodies with their capacity to float through the air, can hardly be understood literally as raised flesh and bone!

We ought also note here, that despite the physicality of the resurrection in this passage, the destination of Christ's resurrection is directly to heaven from whence he will come at the eschaton, to save both the living and the dead, who likewise be resurrected, or in the case of the living, translated to heaven. (1 Thess 4:16) This, however, was not to be the end of Paul's understanding of Jesus' resurrection.

The Pauline understanding of the resurrection is most clearly and fully enunciated in his first letter to the Corinthian church. First, as I have already stated, he claims to 'have seen the Lord,' (1 Cor 9:1) though in this he is clearly speaking of the resurrected Lord, for he never makes any reference to having met Jesus in his lifetime. This experience of the resurrected Lord, Paul claims, gives him authority as an apostle, therefore enabling him to pass on revealed truths that he has received directly from this Christ resurrected to glory. This claim to authority through revelation is distinct from elsewhere, where he makes comment in his name only rather than claiming authority from the Lord. (1 Cor 7:12) A few chapters later, he again lays down authoritative prescriptions for the observance of the Eucharist, when he speaks of these being 'received from the (resurrected) Lord.' (1 Cor 11:23) Likewise, he again claims such authority when speaking of the death and resurrection of Christ in the chapter of this letter, central to his resurrection understanding, I Corinthians 15. There he commences his argument, 'I delivered to you as of first importance what I also received, that Christ died for our sins in accordance with the scriptures, that he was buried, that he was raised on the third day in accordance with the scriptures.' (1 Cor 15:3-4) We need, of course, to keep in mind when Paul claims the authority of 'the scriptures' for his view, he is speaking of the Jewish Scriptures, there being yet no Christian scriptures. Passages that the learned rabbi would have in mind, foreshadowing the resurrection of Jesus, would likely be those I have above noted, 'You have not given me up to Sheol, or let thy godly one see the pit,' (Ps 16:10) 'sit at my right hand, till I make your enemies your footstool,' (Ps 110:1) 'I shall not die, but I shall live, and recount the deeds of the Lord. The Lord has chastened me severely but has not given me over to death.' (Ps 118:17-18) As found, we know that these passages originally had no reference to Jesus, having been written centuries before, concerning things of an immediate context, so the appeal to them carries little weight for us. Rabbinic thinking, however, was different. They, using the method of midrash, combed the scriptures, seeking such passages as a type of proof text, so to give veracity to a current event. Indeed, they shaped the current event by those passages, regarding the reliability of scripture more highly than their own memories or reminiscences. The Christian writers, themselves Jewish, were no different.

For Paul, the resurrected Christ could not be en-fleshed, and he reiterates this over and over in this chapter. He even argues that to believe in an earthly bodily resurrection is to be 'foolish.' (1 Cor 15:35) Here, he perhaps still as a rabbi, has in mind some of those rabbinic views crudely seeing the resurrection as a rehabilitation of our earthly bodies. Whereas earlier, there is some ambiguity concerning his understanding of the physicality or otherwise, of the resurrection being, as we found in examining 1 Thessalonians, it seems now he rejects such literal understandings. Celestial bodies, he charg.es, are of a different order altogether. (1 Cor 15:40-41) Thus, what is raised is of a different order from a 'perishable' earthly body. 'What is sown is perishable, what is raised is imperishable... It is sown a physical body, it is raised a spiritual body.' (1 Cor 15:42-44, 53-54, Phil 3:21) The new person resurrected like Jesus, in whose image they will be, is not born of earth but of heaven. (1 Cor 15:47-49) In order to firmly conclude his argument Paul states, 'flesh and blood cannot inherit the kingdom of God, nor does the perishable inherit the imperishable.' (1 Cor 15:50) Paul's writings with their often deprecatory view of 'the flesh,' could seemingly find no room for such a crudely physical resurrection.

Yet, a form of bodily resurrection there must be, for the Jews, unlike the Greeks, had no separate soul or spirit from the body, and Paul coming from that strong Jewish background, would be unable to conceive of a resurrection form without it being in an embodied, even if spiritually embodied form. (1 Cor 15:44) Clearly however, with Paul that physical resurrection has become not of literal bone and muscle, as it would later become. Such a mystical body, rather than a crude physical body of the resurrected Christ, also had the advantage that it served to allow the Christian to be incorporated into it. Even while still living, those in Christ were 'not in the flesh, but in the Spirit,' (Rom: 8:9-10) this making sense, given that 'The Lord is Spirit.' (2 Cor 3:17) This incorporation of the Christian into this mystical body of Christ is a constant theme in Paul's writings. (1 Cor 15:20-23, Rom 8:22-23) Needless to say, one could hardly be incorporated into a literal physical bone and muscle body! Likewise, the beneficiaries of Christ's resurrection will also be bodily raised, (2 Cor 5:1-4) but given that they will be incorporated into Christ, this can hardly be in crude material form. Clearly, with this view of the resurrection body, there could be no room in Paul's understanding for the resurrected en-fleshed Jesus back to earth of the later tradition!

When the resurrected Christ is revealed to the earth, he is revealed directly from heaven in non-en-fleshed revelatory form. Thus, when Paul speaks of appearances to Cephas (Peter), 'to the twelve,' 'to the five hundred,' and 'to James [and] all the apostles,' these appearances are of the same order as that made to him, to which they are directly compared. (1 Cor 15:5-8)[2] From the earliest time of his writing, Paul clearly conceived of the resurrection as revelatory in nature. Thus, in the letter to the Galatians he speaks of Jesus being revealed to him, (Gal 1:16) the word used, speaking of an epiphany or revelation.

What do we find, or more correctly do not find, in Paul's writings? There is no resurrection in en-fleshed form. Paul does speak of a resurrected body, (Rom 8:11, 23) but it is clear that this body is one very much transformed by the indwelling of the Spirit. The body, though not understood as being in essence evil in Paul, nonetheless in resurrection will be transformed. (Phil 3:21) That transformation is not however, the putting off of this body as something evil, but rather of further 'clothing' it,'so that the mortal may be swallowed up by life.' (2 Cor 5: 2-5) The untransformed body of 'Adam' is destined for the 'dust,' but the new spiritual body is bound for 'heaven.' Just as we inherited the physical body of Adam from dust with its end there, so we inherit that body, come not from dust, but from heaven

---

[2] Given that such a widespread appearance to 500 would seem to be a very strong testimony to the veracity of the resurrection, it is strange it is never again used. A widespread theory is that the events to do with the day of Pentecost, with the reception of the Holy Spirit as described in Acts 2 speak of this same event, it being asserted that Luke has artificially separated the resurrection event and the reception of the Holy Spirit.

having its end there (1 Cor 15: 47-50) In this there is no denigration of the physical, more so a recognition of its limitations. Of course Paul is unable to detail what this resurrection body will actually be as clearly he had no experience of such and thus so the concept is incomprehensible to him (as it is indeed to us) so he is confined to stating what it is not. He can only claim then that it is something which lies in continuity with our physical body but is clothed by the Holy Spirit with a spiritual essence which transforms it.

Understanding resurrection as a vindication of Jesus' way, Paul has no need of a physical resurrection back to the earth, but rather the power of the vindication is in that Jesus was taken to heaven to be with God and this, rather than a half-way house resurrection back to the earth, therefore being subject again to mortality and the will of his opponents, represented the strongest vindication for Paul. Peter speaks likewise in the earliest Christian sermon we have recorded in Acts 3. In the sermon there he speaks of Jesus after his crucifixion, 'whom heaven must receive until the time for establishing all that God spoke by the mouth of his holy prophets of old.' (Acts 3:21) It was only from heaven that Jesus could come again in the triumphant sign of his vindication to bring judgment upon the earth. This is particularly interesting as Acts is the writing of Luke, and Luke as we shall see, is the gospel writer most strongly identified with having Jesus resurrected in corporeal form back to earth. Yet, in this sermon he has Peter, in the earliest of all Christian sermons, give no mention of the type of corporeal earthly resurrection we most identify with Luke.

Paul seems to be here concerned only with resurrection for those 'in Christ.' No mention is made of those who are not in such state when they die. Even with his Jewish background he says nothing of judgement of the evil in Sheol or Gehenna. Omission does not indicate that he did not believe in such, but does show that it is not something of interest to him.

Paul understands Christ's resurrection as the first stage of a general resurrection, (1 Cor 15:23, Col 1:8) which guarantees the believer's future resurrection, (1 Cor 15:17-20, 1 Thess 4:14- 16) with the believer's resurrection happening by the same power which raised Jesus, (1 Cor 6:14, 2 Cor 4:14) Christ's resurrection being the first fruits of a general resurrection (1 Cor 15:20) is instrumental in bringing that believers' resurrection, (Rom 8:11, 1 Cor 15:21-22) for which it is the essential cause. (Romans 4:25 cf 1 Peter 3:21) It also serves as a metaphor for the spiritual experience of believers, (Rom 6:4, Phil 3:10, Col 2:12-13, 3:1-3) this line of thought continuing in the pseudo-Pauline tradition. (Eph 2:5-6)[3]

Though resurrection takes place in Christ, there is still a dimension of it yet to come at the eschaton, with the return of Christ. (1 Thess 4:4) At that point those believers still living, will instantly be raptured to the heavens. (1 Thess 4:16, 1 Cor 15:51-52)

The nature of Christ's resurrection in Paul has two other aspects, which may surprise us. First, given his direct resurrection to heaven there is, clearly, no need for a separate ascension. Second, Christ is the passive recipient of the resurrection enacted by God, rather than the actor of his own resurrection. (Rom 6:4, 10:9, 1 Cor 15:15, 2 Cor 13:4) These things, the ascension, and Christ's self-raising, which have become normative in the Christian understanding of the resurrection, find no testimony in the earliest layer of tradition we possess.

As said, that Jesus' resurrection is not understood in a crude physical manner in Paul's writings, does not mean that it is any less real. For Paul its essential reality is found in its tremendous effects. It is the means by which Christ is able to have spiritual presence with the believers, while also affirms his lordship. (1 Cor 15:44-45, 50, Rom 1:4)

Interestingly, there are only two writers in the Christian Scriptures who claim to have seen the glorified Lord, Paul, (1 Cor 9:1, 15:8, Acts: 9:3-8, 22:6-11, 26:12-18) and John of the Revelation, (Rev 1:10-18) and for both, these are clearly revelatory non-physical appearances. The experience of Christ as risen is clearly then, not necessarily tied to his corporeal resurrection!

Let us turn now to the earliest of our gospels, Mark, and look at the resurrection understanding we find there. As with Paul, so in Mark we will

---

[3] The genuine Pauline epistles are generally held to be, I Thessalonians (c. 50 CE), Galatians (c. 53 CE), 1 Corinthians (c. 53-54 CE), Philippians (c. 55 CE), Philemon (c. 55 CE), 2 Corinthians (c. 55-56 CE) and Romans (c. 57 CE). There is debate over whether Colossians and 2 Thessalonians are genuinely Pauline, while it is almost universally accepted that 1 Timothy, 2 Timothy, Titus, and Ephesians, are pseudepigraphic.

be greatly surprised! In Mark's gospel proper we find only eight verses out of a total of 665 that describe the event central to Christian understanding. These few verses are found as we would expect at the end of the gospel, Mark 16:1-8, but rather than acting as a culmination represent a total anti-climax. Some women find the tomb of Jesus empty, flee in shock and tell no one about it! We find nowhere in this gospel of anyone believing in the resurrection, except the women who are more terrified by what they have witnessed than anything else, and who when instructed by the angelic figure to bear witness to the resurrection by 'telling the disciples and Peter that he is going ahead of you to Galilee where you will see him,' (Mark 16:7) instead 'said nothing to anyone for they were afraid.' (Mark 16:8) That is hardly, need it be said, a note of the 'Hallelujah Chorus' to conclude upon! While the women, as in all the gospels, are the first witnesses to the resurrection, interesting in terms of their subsequent treatment by the church to this day, in this case they are not here held up as examples of what to do with the testimony of the resurrection, for they keep tight-lipped about it.[4]

This is not to judge the women, who, after all, rather than the men, are the first witnesses to the resurrection. Lest any of the male apostles should feel that they would respond differently, the women's response is the same as that made by them when faced with the same type of experience challenging their reality: Jesus' walking on the water, (Mark 6:50, 52) the occasion they are short of bread and Jesus refers to the leaven of both the Pharisees and Herod, (Mark 8:14-21) and on the three occasions when Jesus says he must journey to Jerusalem to suffer and die. (Mark 8:32-33, 9:6, 32, 10:33) On those three episodes of Jesus' speaking of his suffering death the apostles' egotistical actions make abundantly clear their total misunderstanding.

---

[4] It would appear certain that women were indeed understood to be the first witnesses of the resurrection. This is affirmed in all four gospels. It would hardly be likely that the increasingly patriarchal church would have constructed such a story, which must have been an embarrassment to them. The knowledge of the tradition, however, was too strong for it to be suppressed. The best they can do is make the women poor witnesses as in Mark's gospel, or seen to be tellers of an 'idle tale,' in Luke, almost certainly an allusion to women's legal inability to testify at that time. (Luke 24:12) The stories further ring true in that the apostles are made to appear as non-believers in the resurrection. This again would hardly be a construction, given their increasingly prestigious position in the church.

Such fear as exhibited by the women is entirely natural and is often associated with great epiphanies such as this. As we have seen it was certainly the response of Peter, James and John at the Transfiguration. The young, clearly meant to be angelic man's admonition, not to fear is associated with such epiphanies not only in the biblical tradition but more generally in antiquity, is seen also in Luke's account of the angelic chorus' appearance to the shepherds announcing the birth of Jesus. (Luke 2:10) Rudolf Otto, the early 20th century theologian and comparative religion scholar, with a particular interest in phenomenology, especially the religious experience, spoke of such experience and epiphany at depth defining it as 'mysterium tremendum et fascinans,' that which mystifies and fascinates but is also terrifying.

So shocked was the early church by the lack of triumphalism in this gospel there were some who appended endings to it, to better reflect the glory they believed it should have concerning the resurrection. Most of our English editions of the scriptures give us two of these later endings, making it abundantly clear when they do so, that they indeed are later attachments. (Mark 16: 9-20)

Certainly there is no word in Mark's gospel on any of those who later were to become recognized as the apostles believing the resurrection. They simply just don't make an appearance, it left only to the women to be the recipients. These women represent the continuity between the crucifixion, which they had also witnessed, (Mark 15: 40, 47) and the resurrection, (Mark 16:1) the names of both Marys being specifically mentioned, with added detail that the second one of them was 'the mother of James and Salome.'

The whole Marcan resurrection episode is very low key, there being no angelic appearances (though as we have seen the 'young man' is clearly meant to be so understood), nor earthquakes or swooning guards, 'like dead men.' The empty tomb in Mark inspires not faith but rather fear, while even the statement made by a 'young man,' 'he is risen,' one of the earliest of the Christian creeds, finds no faith acceptance. The appearance of this figure becomes more elevated in the succeeding gospels, so to make his supernatural nature clearer. In Mark this figure proclaims the resurrection but the passive voice used in this proclamation makes clear that Jesus is a passive recipient of God's resurrection power, rather than the active instigator of his own resurrection. The understanding of he himself, being the active instigator of his resurrection will come later in this evolving tradition.

The women's failure to testify concerning the resurrection makes sense, however, as their prime experience has only been that of an empty grave, and though later the empty grave would be used as an apologetic, it is never so used in the gospels. Here it only leads to fear, while in Luke's gospel those traveling the road to Emmaus are only confused by it, (Luke 24:13-33) while in John's Gospel, the main conclusion is that the body has been moved, (John 20:2) while the manner of the grave-clothes thus left does not compel belief. (John 20:6-8) For those of us brought up with the idea that the empty grave lies at the very heart of the evidence for the resurrection, this no doubt comes as a shock. The empty tomb in the gospels is used not as proof for resurrection, but rather to show its nature; one being clearly bodily. Belief in the resurrection already being assumed, these details serve not as evidence for the event, which after all is already believed, but rather to indicate the type of resurrection. Thus so, the empty tomb and the grave-clothes are meant to be understood as being the left 'evidence' of that style of physical resurrection.

The instruction given to the women to pass onto the disciples, is to tell them to go to Galilee. Galilee as the place for the resurrection, would seem to be the older of the location traditions, the other being Jerusalem. Jerusalem of course lay at the heart of the Jewish understanding, and given that the earliest Christians were Jewish and regarded Jesus, including his resurrection, as the fulfillment of their (Hebrew) scriptures and tradition, in time, the resurrection location naturally increasingly became located in Jerusalem. The Jerusalem tradition would be strengthened with the increased emphasis on the empty tomb and earthly appearances of the risen Lord at the tomb and elsewhere in the city. By the end of the gospel tradition, as we shall see, Galilee as a location for the resurrection will be entirely marginalized, Jerusalem entirely becoming the place associated with the miracle. In Mark's gospel however, with the Galilee tradition still primary, the disciples are told, 'go to Galilee; there you will see him, as he told you,' (Mark 16:7) with the last part of that statement, 'as he told you' referring back to words spoken by Jesus at his last supper on the eve of his death. (Mark 14:28) Interestingly, there in the following verse Peter made a statement full of bravado of how 'even though they all fall away, I will not.' (Mark 14:29) Of course, we know his bravado does not succeed in saving him from a humbling failure. In the Marcan resurrection instructions Peter is therefore rehabilitated, his name being specially mentioned. 'Go, tell his disciples, and Peter, that he is going before you to Galilee.' Peter, already martyred, is, as early as the time of Mark's Gospel, understood to be a much too important figure in the infant church for his shortcomings, which clearly were too well known to be expunged, to be left without his name rehabilitated.

Though in Mark's Gospel the Galilee tradition still holds prime place, the Jerusalem tradition is already making its mark, the empty tomb story locating the disciples at the time of the resurrection, as being in that city. The empty tomb story is also the first step in the understanding that Jesus' resurrection is to be understood as literally physical in nature.

The next gospel we will examine is that of Matthew. He in his resurrection account, as in the rest of his gospel, uses much of Mark's material, but also adds his own. With Matthew we find ourselves some 55 years after the events being described. The church is still primarily Jewish, with these Jewish believers in Jesus as the expected Messiah under increasing pressure from the rest of the Jewish community. That Jewish community had just passed through catastrophe and was seeking to recover, given all which was central to it, the Temple and Jerusalem, had been destroyed by the Romans, following the Jewish revolt of 66-70 CE. Understandably the preservation of their identity, including that most central to it, the orthodox expression of faith, had become crucial for the Jewish community. That orthodoxy was however, now greatly changed. Given the lack of a temple in which to carry out the old sacrificial cult, synagogue worship with its emphasis on the Scripture, particularly the Torah, the first five books of the Jewish scriptures, believed to have written by Moses while under divine inspiration, was now the heart of Jewish faith and cultural expression. This community viewed with increasing disdain those who did not hold the Torah in the same esteem as they did. Had not Jesus, and did not his successors, relativize the Torah? No doubt they could point to Paul and other figures in the Jesus community, who clearly did that. Further, were not these followers of Jesus admitting to their ranks the Goyim (Gentiles), those who had just wreaked disaster upon them?

Thus relationships among the Jewish community between those who saw Jesus as the Messiah, the Jesus Jews, and those who did not, which earlier had been cordial enough, those believing in Jesus still attending the synagogue, began to be increasingly strained. Thus, in Matthew's Gospel we have a most disparaging picture of the Jewish community, with the contemporary situation of friction between the Jewish followers of Jesus, and those, the majority, who did not follow within that community, being projected back to the time of Jesus so that 'the Jews' are held to be primarily responsible for Jesus' execution, while the Roman Pilate, washing his hands, is 'innocent of this man's blood.' (Matt 27:24) Matthew even has the Jewish crowd spontaneously, unrealistically clearly, cry out in unison, 'his blood be upon us and our children.' (Matt 27:25) Little comment needs to be made as to the disastrous consequences of 'the Jews' as a whole being made the perpetrators of Jesus' death. The story of virulent anti-Semitism within Christianity has run deep, culminating in the horrendous events of the Nazi regime. That regime's practices only gained traction however, due to the very long anti-Semitic attitudes in the church.

In Matthew's gospel then the Jewish people are understood to force the supposedly reluctant hand of the Romans to have Jesus executed. The reality, likely would have been that parts of the Jewish leadership were involved, but such leadership collaboration is something in common with almost all occupied peoples. Probably such collaboration came about both, because the leadership was doing quite well out of the arrangement cut with the occupier, but also because they recognized the reality of the strength of the occupying power, therefore knew that any disturbance was almost certainly going to lead to a catastrophic result for the Jewish nation, with a resultant more repressive manner of occupation, as indeed it would some 30 years later. Therefore, it was sensible policy to work with the occupier to 'keep the peace.'

Matthew's trial scene with the supposed cry of the crowd, 'Let him be crucified' (Matt 27:15-23) is again Matthew's creation, reflective of that later issue of enmity between the Jesus Jews and those who held to the more orthodox line, which frames his gospel, and as such has no real historical base. Jesus' dispute is not with the crowd, but rather with the leadership of the community. The actual truth comes out in the same gospel when we read that the authorities at the time of Passover, a time when Jerusalem was filled with the common people, 'tried to arrest him but feared the multitudes, because they held him to be a prophet.' (Matt 21:45-46) Being popular with the crowds, Jesus is able to discourse with them concerning the corruption of the leadership, 'Blind fools…whitewashed tombs… sons of those who murdered the prophets.' (Matthew 23) He is hardly likely speaking such to a crowd that in unison would soon bay for his death before Pilate! Lest it be said, that public opinion had suddenly changed by the time of his arrest we still find at that time the collaborating leadership seeking to arrest Jesus, but fearing the crowds not doing so 'during the feast, [when such huge numbers charged by nationalist fervor were present] lest there be tumult among the people.' (Matt 26:3-5) Instead, the act is done secretly at night. A little detective work of reading between the lines usually sees the truth out! There was no enmity between Jesus and popular Judaism. Indeed it seems the opposite was true, that Jesus was admired by the crowds for his critique of the Jewish establishment, such actions as his overturning of the tables of the exploitative money-changers in the Temple likely going down well with the common populace. He is a radical prophet in a long line of such, representative of a rich Jewish prophetic tradition. Jesus thus stands within the Jewish tradition, but like the prophets of old, is not afraid to critique it when he judges it as having become corrupted, especially among the leadership.

Just as the antipathy at the time of writing of Matthew's gospel between that segment of that smaller part Jewish community, who making up the majority of the infant church, believed in Jesus as Messiah, and those who did not, framed the Passion narrative, the same antipathy likewise also frames the resurrection narrative in this gospel. That account begins with a prelude, peculiar to Matthew, of the Jewish leadership, even before any resurrection has happened, going to Pilate and asking that the tomb of Jesus be secured for they "remember how that impostor said, while he was still alive, 'After three days I will rise again'." (Matt 27:63) They supposedly do this in order to make it impossible for the disciples to go and steal his body away and then claim 'he has risen from the dead.' (Matt 27:64) This is precisely what the Jewish community at the time of Matthew's writing, was charging those among them who believed in Jesus of doing! It is hardly likely as such to reflect any real event. The Jewish leadership after-all would have other preoccupations on the day, in which they, according to the text, were negotiating with Pilate, it being the Passover Sabbath.

On such a day they certainly would not have wished to risk ritually defiling themselves by going to Pilate's palace. This whole passage is a construction by Matthew designed to rebut the charges, contemporary with his writing, leveled by the Jewish community against those who believed in Jesus, that they had stolen the body and made out that he had risen. The ground is being prepared to say that in spite of these charges, presented as historical precautions taken at the time, the resurrection is a reality. Only lies and falsehoods, concocted by the Jews, according to Matthew, can stand in the way of its evidence. In reality however it would appear that it is Matthew himself who is twisting the truth in creating this story.

In composing his resurrection account Matthew draws from a story found in the Hebrew Scriptures. In that story Joshua, of which the name Jesus is the Greek form, placed a stone with guards across a cave in which he was holding five kings. (Josh 10:16-18) In the Jewish lectionary that passage would have been read during the month of Nissan, just after Passover, that time being when these events to do with Jesus' resurrection were taking place. Elsewhere we read of Daniel, imprisoned by a stone rolled across in a cave of lions, escaping alive unharmed (Dan 6:17) with an angel, as here, present. (Daniel 6:22) Again, in Daniel another epiphany of angels brings a response which is paralleled in Matthew's resurrection account, with Daniel's angel having 'the appearance of lightning' causing 'great trembling' to come upon those guarding Daniel. (Dan 10:6-7) These accounts again represent classic examples of midrash, whereby the veracity of the current event is proven by its being paralleled to one from within the sacred tradition. As earlier said this was a much higher form of proof for the gospel writers than mere eye- witnessing, which after all could be mistaken. Hopefully by now it is clear just how much midrash shapes the ongoing tradition in both the Hebrew and Christian Scriptures. Matthew is aiming to show us that nothing, especially the 'pernicious acts and lying schemes of the Jews,' can get in the way of God's great plan in Jesus. In this gospel that same idea is already in the infancy narrative with the scheming actions of Herod. We now see it again at the end of Jesus' life with the 'chief priests and the Pharisees.'

Matthew heightens the spectacular nature of the whole resurrection story, that commencing even before we get to Jesus' resurrection itself. While we must wait until the third day after his death for Jesus' resurrection, his death itself commences the time of general resurrection, for at the very moment of his expiration, 'the tombs also were opened and many bodies of the saints who had fallen asleep were raised, and coming out of the tombs after his resurrection they went into the holy city and appeared to many.' (Matt 27:52-53) Nothing is said in this strange schema as to what those bodies risen from the tomb did in the interim between the crucifixion when they rose, and the resurrection of Jesus, when they decided to visit the city. In any event it must have been an entirely strange and terrifying event! This account almost certainly draws on the metaphorical resurrection account in Ezekiel 37 especially the words, 'when I open your graves and bring you up from them... you will live.' (Ezek 37:13-14)

When we get to Jesus' actual resurrection the young man in white, whose apparel hints at his supernatural status in Mark, now has that supernatural status made explicit, becoming in this gospel, an angel with a fantastic 'appearance like lightning, and raiment white as snow,' (Matt 28:3) who rolls back the stone, upon which he sits in triumph. This description of the angel is clearly shaped by the great apocalyptic figure in Daniel. (Dan 7:9, 10:6 cf Rev 1:14-15, 10:1) That heightening will continue literally with the angel figure(s) so that by the time we get to the non-canonical Gospel of Peter, the angels, who accompany Jesus from the tomb, have 'heads... reaching heaven but that of him (Jesus) who led them by the hand surpassing the heavens.' (Gos. Pet. 39-40)

Matthew likes to speak of great supernatural intervention in his ever more fantastic resurrection account, beginning with the resurrection of the dead at the time of Jesus' death, as we have seen, but also associated with Jesus' resurrection itself, where we read of a great earthquake and an angel descending to roll the stone away from the tomb. (Matt 28:2)

We next have the women, who in Mark's gospel showed such fear, arrive at the tomb. This time they are countenanced against that fear by the 'angel of the Lord,' and though they 'depart quickly from the tomb with fear' (and who could blame them with all they supposedly witnessed!), they leave with 'great joy,' and unlike in Mark's account, 'go quickly and tell the disciples that he has risen from the dead.' (Matt 28:1-7)

Before they leave the garden, however, they encounter the risen Jesus. This clearly for the first time is a physical manifestation of the crucified one now directly raised back to earth, rather than to the heavens with that physicality being testified by their taking hold of his feet. (Matt 28:9-10) This understanding of Jesus being resurrected directly back to the earth on the third day, belief which would become Christian orthodoxy, thus does not emerge then until about 85CE, some 55 years after the actual events described, and here it is only very temporary before he ascends! The story of the women taking hold of Jesus' feet does not reflect any historical event so much as being yet another example of midrash, paralleling one where some Shumanite women take hold of Elisha's feet, an episode also linked to a resurrection experience. (2 Kgs 4:27)

Then we are told of how it is the non-believing Jews who bribe the guards to say that, 'the disciples stole the body.' These are the guards of course supposedly placed there in order to oppose Jesus followers being involved in perjury by their stealing his body. The guards, derelict in their very simple duty, now confirm that the very thing that caused them to be placed there in the first place has indeed happened; the disciples came and stole the body. Perjury, which was supposedly going to be carried out by the followers of Jesus, is now declared by Matthew, to have been carried out by those opposing them! It is not Jesus' followers, but rather 'the Jews' who are liars and manipulators. Their lying and cover-up, all accompanied by acceptance of a bribe, (Matt 28:11-15) is contrasted with speaking of truth and subsequent proclamation by Jesus' followers. (Matt 28:16-20)

The resurrection story again moves on. As instructed, the now eleven disciples go 'to Galilee, to the mountain to which Jesus had directed them.' The appearance here is clearly of the older revelatory type, mountains universally being the place of such revelations. In this account Jesus clearly has come down from where he has been directly resurrected to the heavens, not climbed the mountain as a resuscitated corpse. This mountain experience is of the same genre as that described in chapter 17 of this gospel where Jesus is 'transfigured before them' while Moses and Elijah appear from heaven. Matthew has a particular liking for mountains as places of revelation. (Matt 4:8, 5:1, 8:1, 14:23, 15:29, 17:1, 21:1) This episode, being linked to Galilee, and also of the revelatory type, clearly represents an earlier layer of the unfolding resurrection tradition, which will as we have found, increasingly emphasize the physicality of its nature, and also its placement in Jerusalem. I shall return to that ongoing geographical movement when we examine Luke's resurrection account.

As to the main actor in the resurrection, Jesus is still the recipient of God's resurrection power, the same passive voice being used, as in Mark's gospel. The movement toward Jesus being the author of his own resurrection, rather than being the recipient of a resurrection orchestrated by God, will reflect an increasingly elevated Christology concerning Jesus, that Christology finally developing to a point, where by the fourth century, Jesus was considered fully divine, that becoming established as Christian orthodoxy.

Of prime importance in Matthew's gospel, however, is the change to the locality of Jesus' resurrection, it being no longer to the heavens, from which he could appear in a revelatory manner, but rather to the earth on which this physicality was manifested. While in Matthew we find this changing understanding as to the nature of the resurrection, the older revelatory tradition, as we have seen, still survives. The two traditions, the older of Jesus resurrected directly to heaven from which he makes revelatory appearances to the disciples now returned to Galilee, is mixed with that which is newer, in which the resurrection becomes physical in nature, to the earth, with a specific location in Jerusalem.

The gospel ends with Jesus command 'to go therefore and make disciples of all nations, baptizing them in the name of the Father and of the Son and of the Holy Spirit, teaching them to observe all that I have commanded you.' (Matt 28:20) They do so by 'all the authority in heaven and on earth,' which having been given to Jesus, he now passes to them, with his everlasting presence, 'to the close of the age.' These words may be drawn from Daniel 7:14. There, the 'son on man' figure has that same authority, an authority which is to extend over 'all nations.' By such words we may conclude with the observation that the Jewish Messiah has now been elevated to be the cosmic Christ!

Matthew has taken the resurrection tradition and literalized it. The resurrected Jesus before this, present in heaven as an eschatological or end time sign of hope for all things, is now placed within history.[5] As well

---

[5] Eschatology literally means a discourse on the final things. It is central to biblical

as becoming increasingly made literal, the story is also being heightened in form. Thus, the stone which we are simply told in Mark's gospel was 'rolled back,' is now, we are told, rolled back accompanied by a great earthquake 'by an angel of the Lord, descended from heaven.' The 'young man sitting on the right' has now overtly become an angel now sitting in triumph upon the stone rolled back, while the entry into the tomb, left ambiguous by Mark as to whether the women or anyone else ever did enter, now becomes a crucial piece of evidence against the contemporary Jewish polemic. Leslie Houlden speaking of the resurrection in his, 'Backward into Light' judges Matthew as spoiling Mark's purity, turning mystery and ambiguity as particularly represented in Jesus' cry of dereliction, 'My God, my God why have you forsaken me?' (Mark 15:34) into something explicit, public and indisputable. Faith he notes is no longer a gift but rather is bludgeoned out of his readers by apocalyptic portents, angelophony and explicit appearances.[6]

The major problem with the increasing physicality of Jesus' resurrection and placing it back to the earth, is that it increasingly begins to look like a bodily resuscitation, raising two issues: the first is the question as to whether Jesus actually ever died, an idea I reject on the basis, as said, that the Romans did know how to execute successfully, but none the less left open when the resurrection begins to look like a resuscitation, and second, that as a resuscitated physical being Jesus is still subject to the decay of aging and finally death. As such the triumph of the resurrection is muted. I conclude therefore with Robert Morgan, 'The gospels do not intend to relate a resuscitation. There is no question of Jesus dying again. A physical resuscitation looks dangerously like resuscitation, and invites

---

understanding, which sees history moving toward a perfection, which ultimately lies outside it. Thus, Jews looked forward to the coming Messiah to inaugurate the perfect age, marked by peace, justice, cosmic harmony, love and compassion. Jerusalem would be that sign of those things to all peoples, who will come from all nations. This view is seen in Matthew's gospel where at the point of Jesus' resurrection, 'the tombs were opened, and bodies of the saints, who had fallen asleep were raised.' (Matt 27:52) In those events the final age has already been inaugurated. For Christians, orthodoxy became that the eschatological age has already commenced with the coming of the Messiah. He came demonstrating the fullness of the presence of that time, but also as an anticipation of its presence for all. Those bonded to him already share in that perfection and are called to be anticipatory signs for the whole of creation still groaning in travail.' (Rom 8:19-23)

[6] J.L. Houlden Backward into Light: The Passion and Resurrection of Jesus According to Matthew and Mark, London : S.C.M. 1983.

the rationalist explanation that Jesus did not really die on the cross. It is better avoided.[7] This increasing literalizing of the resurrection, as being understood increasingly more like a physical resuscitation, would continue into the second century with not only the resurrection of Jesus, but the general resurrection, increasingly associated with actual flesh and bone.

Let us turn to Luke, the third of our gospels. Luke may be the only Gentile writer in the Christian scriptures, though as said earlier this is hotly debated. Even if Luke is Jewish he is the one who has most escaped the boundaries of that tradition. It is his gospel that traces the genealogy of Jesus not to Abraham, the founder of the Jewish nation, as does Matthew, but to Adam, the first born among humans, while Luke alone contains the story, which breaks, I believe, most radically through Jewish exclusivism, the Good Samaritan. (Luke 10:29-37) Luke is also more prone to give us instances of Jesus' breaking the Sabbath laws by his healing activities, (Luke 6:6-11, 13:10-17, 14:1-6) while in his sequel, the book of Acts, he gives us the only account of Peter, by that time seen by many to be the founder and leader of the church, breaking the kosher laws, (Acts 10:9-16) before concluding, God shows no partiality to any nation. (Acts 10:34-35)

With Luke we are now further removed from the actual Jesus events in their Jewish context by perhaps another 25 years, the church becoming increasingly Gentile.[8] Different, more universal influences, are being

---

[7] Robert Morgan, Flesh is Precious: The Significance of Luke 24:36-43 in Essays in honour of Leslie Houlden, eds Stephen Barton and Graham Stanton. Society for the Propagation of Christian Knowledge, London, 1994: 12

[8] It is easily overlooked that all the earliest followers of Jesus were Jewish. Indeed the first major debate in the church concerned the question as to whether the gospel had any relevance at all to Gentiles, or whether it should be contained within Judaism. During the time of the writing of the Christian Scriptures many argued that it was something to be contained as a reform movement within Judaism, James and Matthew being representative of this group, while others believed it represented something radically new, breaking free of the constraints of Judaism, Paul being the champion of this group. Thus, while Matthew has Jesus announce, 'Think not that I have come to abolish the Law and the prophets; I have come not to abolish them but to fulfill them. For truly I say to you, till heaven and earth pass away not an iota of the Law (Torah) will pass from the Law' and has Jesus actually intensify the Law,' (Matt 5: 17-48) Paul views the Law (Torah) negatively, as something already finished. (Gal 2:16, 21, 3: 23-26)

exercised upon it, and in response the church begins to present its beliefs in a manner more amenable to that wider world.

Of particular importance as an influence in Luke is the use of mythology, associated with heroic figures present in the surrounding mythologies. A constant theme within mythological stories was the image of the heroic figure being snatched up, or raptured to heaven, from where they would materialize from time to time, in order to assist those carrying on their work. This was not entirely absent in the scriptural tradition, with both Elijah and Enoch being so snatched to heaven, but in Luke's Gospel it is possible to see this mainly Gentile divine hero mythological image most strongly shaping the writer's understanding of the resurrection.

Luke further emphasizes the physicality of the resurrection, it continuing to become ever more so in nature, while being back to earth. He also further objectifies the resurrection by giving proof of its occurrence. Let us now examine this story as presented by Luke.

We commence with a post-crucifixion pre-resurrection account found in the conclusion of chapter 23: 50-56. There, we find the tomb identified for the first time with Joseph of Arimathea, who had taken the body, as well as being informed that the tomb had never been used. As such we could conclude that it was indeed Joseph's own tomb. The women, who had come with him from Galilee, we are told, followed Joseph, saw the tomb in which the body was laid, and presumably saw the stone rolled across to seal it. They then return to prepare spices and ointments to anoint the body of Jesus. The intense, absolute finality of all of this, is clearly meant to prepare us for the miraculous empty tomb.

The actual resurrection account begins with the women, who having prepared the spices and then rested on the Sabbath, returning to the tomb, which they expect surely will be firmly sealed as when they left it. Suddenly however, Luke has that apparent finality broken open. We are told of how on arrival at the tomb, the women find the stone rolled away, and upon entering are perplexed to find the body missing. Their perplexity seemingly only lasts a moment before they are told by 'two men standing by them in dazzling apparel,' who ask of them, 'why do you seek the living among the dead?' There is becoming ever less space, as the tradition develops, for mystery and ambiguity within the story. The lingering

Galilee tradition now is cunningly done away with. The previous post-resurrection command to 'go to Galilee' where the resurrection will be witnessed, now becomes 'remember how he told you while he still was in Galilee.' (Luke 24:6) Thus so, the previous locale of the resurrection now becomes only the place of his speaking of it while he was still living. Jerusalem for Luke is the end-point of the ministry of Jesus, and it becomes the beginning place for the ministry of those who follow him. Thus, Luke's gospel ends with the journey of Jesus, who has journeyed from Galilee to the nation's capital, Jerusalem, where the resurrection takes place, followed by his sequel, the Book of Acts, which details the movement of the gospel from that place to the empire's capital, Rome. The apostles, 'the eleven and all the rest', are pulled into the Jerusalem story by being named as being present in that place. That Luke speaks of 'all the rest' might indicate that he knows the original figure of twelve, now reduced to eleven by Judas' actions, is only an artificial one, in order to parallel the twelve Jewish tribes. These 'others' presumably include the women, some of whom we have just heard. Thus, again we catch a glimpse of the reality behind the created façade of the all-male apostolic group. The women however, now with three named, along with 'other women with them,' return to bear witness to the miracle they have experienced, only to be dismissed as carriers of idle gossip by the disbelieving apostles and 'the rest.'

Though it has not yet elicited belief among the apostles, the empty tomb is continually elevated in status, to become a literal testimony for the resurrection. Thus, the angel's statement becomes one that assumes the empty tomb as being proof of the resurrection: 'Why do you seek the living among the dead?' before affirming how Jesus had spoken of how he must be killed, and on the third day rise. (Luke 24:5-7) Later, we will be told by the two on the Emmaus road that others also 'went to the tomb and found it just as the women had said.' (Luke 24:24) While the women's legally unreliable verbal testimony cannot be believed, and is dismissed as 'an idle tale,' (Luke 24:12) the empty tomb is becoming more and more proof of the resurrection.

Next comes a story peculiar to Luke, the story of the Emmaus road. This type of hospitality story is popular in folklore from many places where, in the humble actions of hosting, a person hosts the divine unawares. In such instances the divine one comes to help those following in his path, often in time of need. Tolstoy's story of the cobbler is well known. Elsewhere in the Christian Scriptures we similarly read, 'Do not neglect to show hospitality to strangers, for thereby some have entertained angels unawares.' (Heb 13:2) Once again midrash is at work, for it was Abraham and then Lot we are told, who entertain unknowingly divine messengers, disguised as human beings. (Gen 18:1-9, 19:1-3)

In this story, Luke clearly uses the rapture model, while also emphasizing the physical nature of Jesus' resurrection. Two of the disciples are walking to the nearby village of Emmaus, just outside Jerusalem, when they are 'joined' by a stranger. This joining would hardly seem to be one which is natural, the whole episode pervaded by an air of mystery, with their eyes, we are also told, being 'kept from recognizing him.' (Luke 24:16) As noted, the divine often comes to help in the time of need, and does so here by solving the conundrum of which they were speaking, as to how it could be possible that this Jesus they had followed, and whom they hoped would be, 'the one who would redeem Israel,' had been 'delivered up, condemned to death and crucified.' To make matters worse for them, they add, some of the women, whose testimony, as noted, legally at the time, carried no weight, had come with a story of an empty tomb with angels announcing he had risen. The stranger helps them with this conundrum by telling them that it was 'necessary that the Christ should suffer these things and enter into his glory.' (Luke 24:26) He then shows, 'beginning with Moses and the prophets,' how all the things that Jesus (he himself present as the stranger of course) had done fulfilled the scriptures. In doing this he is employing midrash in classical manner. As found, the Hebrew Scriptures of which the stranger speaks as making the case for the resurrection after three days, are difficult, if not impossible, to find. When they draw near to Emmaus, given that the day is almost spent, the stranger appears to be going further so they invite him to share in their hospitality. At this point, while they are eating the physicality of the resurrection breaks in. While he is 'at table with them, he took the bread and blessed, and broke it, and gave it to them, and their eyes were opened and they recognized him.' (Luke 24:30) This sudden recognition after unseeing, what Aristotle called anagnorisis, is important in classical tragedy.

In this account it is possible to see in the sudden recognition of the Messiah being linked to his sudden physicality, the Lukan project at work, wanting to link proof or recognition of the resurrected Jesus, to his being physically present. Theologically it appears that Luke desires to link the now resurrected glorified one with the crucified suffering one. In order to achieve this, we have in this account a re-enactment of the last supper, celebrated immediately before his crucifixion, with the same words and elements being present. Thus, Jesus takes bread, blesses it and gives it in the same manner as in that supper the night before he died. (Luke 22:19) The suddenly apparent physicality of Jesus, matching his physical presence at the last supper, serves to further show this continuity. There is also a clear Eucharistic connection with thanksgiving, breaking and sharing all present here. Luke also apparently seeks to make clear that there can be no worship of the risen Christ in a cultic manner alone, that can be abstracted from the following of the servant Jesus. That Eucharistic meal before his death, is the Pesach or Passover meal, the celebration of liberation long ago from Egypt and the anticipation of the messianic banquet. As such it challenges those who celebrate it to the equitable sharing of wine and bread, symbolic of the gifts of God, as an anticipation of the sharing of abundance in the messianic reign. Faith must have an ethical perspective in its concern for those for whom Jesus showed concern. Thus so in carrying out the simple act of sharing, these two sojourners have their eyes opened and they see the hereto unseen Jesus. The resurrection is only truly witnessed in such action. Having seen him so, he then suddenly is gone from their sight and they are now left to share that bread with each other. It is almost as if having shown they understand the need to share, the two no longer have need for the presence of Jesus.

It is no coincidence that this happens where hospitality is offered, and over a meal where bread is shared. Their recognition of Jesus may be because he was often at table and they would have had a strong association of Jesus with such table sharing. (Luke 5:29, 7:36, 9:10-17, 11:37,12:37,13:29, 14:1, 8-9, 22:14) Like this table where the stranger is welcomed, the tables of which Jesus spoke, and at which he sat, were always marked by an open commensality. The account may be meant to testify that the disciples have learnt this, and therefore is meant to show that all tables in the church were to be open. This is part then, of Luke's dealing with the question as to whether Gentiles should be accepted fully into the church, a question which greatly vexed the early church, creating enormous conflict.

That sudden disappearance from their sight (Luke 24:31) represents of course a return to the rapture model. The two disciples return to Jerusalem where 'they found the eleven gathered together,' meaning presumably these Emmaus road two were not members of the original twelve, and learn there that the Lord has likewise appeared in a rapturous manner to Simon. Jerusalem is becoming ever more strongly the place at the heart of the resurrection story.

Now follows yet another appearance (Luke 24:36-49), full, like that we have just examined, of both rapture and also physicality, this story paralleling in many ways the Emmaus story. Again, we find the non-recognition of Jesus by followers troubled with their many unresolved questions, the physicality of Jesus emphasized by his partaking food with them, in his explaining the Law and the prophets, and his opening their minds to understand from the Scriptures that it was, 'necessary for the Christ to suffer, and on the third day rise from the dead.' Clearly Luke intended these stories to be read together. The main difference seems to be the markedly lower key telling of the Emmaus story.

Continuing with the narrative we find that while the recipients of the appearance on the road to Emmaus as well as Simon are relating their stories, of the disciples it is said, 'Jesus himself stood among them.' (Luke 24:36) Understandably they suppose they are seeing a spirit, for this is clearly no ordinary, but rather a rapturous, means of his coming into their midst. Luke, however, then suddenly changes tone, emphasizing the physical rather than the rapturous nature of this resurrected Jesus. Thus, the resurrected one challenges them, 'see my hands and my feet, that it is I myself, handle me, and see; for a spirit has not flesh and bones as you see that I have.' (Luke 24:39) This physicality is further reinforced by his asking for and eating broiled fish. He then instructs them all, as he likewise had instructed those on the road, using midrash as evidence, that indeed, 'the Christ should suffer and on the third day rise from the dead.' (Luke 24:46) Both this appearance, with his showing his crucifixion scars and eating broiled fish, and the account of the Emmaus road, are meant to testify to the continuity between the crucified Jesus and the resurrected Christ. Again, we are being shown that there can be no one-sided Christology built around the resurrected one of power, while not being cognizant that this one is the same as that one who was crucified.

This rapture model, which Luke retains alongside his developing physical resurrection emphasis, allows for Christ to be experienced as revelation by his followers upon the earth long after his resurrection and ascension, and Luke makes use of it as such with there being a couple of examples in the Book of Acts. Stephen at the point of martyrdom has a revelation of Jesus, (Acts 7:55-56) while Paul, in a story thrice told, hears Jesus speak while on the road to Damascus. (Acts 9:3-5, 22:6-8, 26:13-15)

The increasing dominance of the Jerusalem tradition is seen with the disciples being countenanced to stay in that city until, 'clothed with power from on high.' (Luke 24:49) The gospel then ends with Christ being raptured from them in the ascension, that now however, taking place in Jerusalem. We have already been prepared for this geographical location in Luke's account of the Transfiguration, where in a story shared by all three synoptics, Luke alone, has Moses and Elijah speak of 'his departure, which he was to accomplish at Jerusalem.' (Luke 9:31) In that account, following Jesus' coming down from the mountain, Luke writes, 'when the days drew near for him to be received up, he set his face to go to Jerusalem,' (Luke 9:51) indicating clearly that this must be the locale for Jesus' in the ascension being 'received up.'

Luke clearly, having Jesus resurrected in such a physical manner to the earth, must have him leave the earth to ascend to the domain proper for divinity, hence the need for the ascension.

In Luke's gospel all these events – the discovery of the empty tomb, the Emmaus road journey, the rapturous appearance of Jesus, the appearance with the disciples at meal, and the ascension – all happen on the same day. Luke will modify this, particularly in regards to the ascension, in his sequel to the gospel, his Book of Acts. There, he will introduce the ascension as taking place 40 days after the resurrection, while also introducing the gift of the Holy Spirit, placing its giving at the time of Pentecost, another ten days later.

Luke's Gospel also removes Jesus' resurrection from its connection with the eschatological, the commencement of a new age. Paul has linked the resurrection of Jesus to the inauguration of that age, (1 Cor 15:20- 27a) Mark has spoken in what I consider to be a deliberate ambiguous nature of how 'you will see him' (Mark 14:28, 16:7), seemingly indicating either the resurrection or the parousia (second coming), but actually I believe meaning both, while Matthew clearly links Jesus' resurrection with both the eschatological resurrection of all (Matt 27:51b-53) and the parousia. (Matt 28:16-20) Luke, however, breaks that eschatological link with the resurrection, understanding it rather as a reversal of the events of Good Friday. That fits with his project of making literal the resurrection in his returning Jesus to the earth, specifically to Jerusalem, the location in which the Good Friday crucifixion events had occurred.

For Luke, as well as reversing the events of Good Friday, the final resurrection means the reversal of all things. This interest in reversal, Luke has made clear from the beginning of his gospel in the Magnificat, from a time even before Jesus' birth, (Luke 1:46-55) and in his oft-used image of the great messianic feast, symbolic of the reign of God at the end of the age, where all things will be reversed. At the feast of the Messiah seating arrangements won't be dependent on one's worldly honor, nor will 'the expected' be invited. Instead those at the table will be 'the poor, maimed, lame and blind.' (Luke 14:7-14) In a society which saw these ailments as a sign of God's displeasure and therefore punishment, this is highly significant. Other very clear examples of this eschatological reversal in this gospel are found in the parable of Lazarus and 'Dives,' and also in his version of the Beatitudes (Luke 6)

Let us now turn to the second of Luke's writings, the Book of Acts.

In his introduction to Acts, Luke alludes to how in his 'first book' he spoke of 'all that Jesus began to do and teach, until the day he was taken up.' (Acts 1:1-2) When he comes to this being 'taken up', however, suddenly the previous chronology changes, for Luke introduces the 'forty days' which will become the marker for the Christian feast of the ascension. (Acts 1:3) As well as representing a chronological change, the ascension represents a change of emphasis. Prior to this, the Christian tradition spoke not of ascension but exaltation, that being associated with the resurrection. (Phil 2:6-14, Heb 1:3-4, Eph 1:20, 1 Tim 3:16, 1 Pet 3:21-22) What Luke does in Acts is to separate the resurrection from the final exaltation to glory, by his introduction of the ascension. That separation is partially present in his gospel where both resurrection and ascension take place on the same day, but is accentuated when the two events are separated by 40 days, as they are in the book of Acts.

Again, midrash is at work with Luke modeling Jesus' ascension to glory on that of Elijah. (2 Kgs 2: 9-12) Between the time of resurrection and exaltation in the ascension, the risen Christ makes a series of rapturous appearances to the believers. (Acts 1:3) At the point of the ascension, Jesus leaves them for good, but does so offering them a divine power to be present with them, this divine power being the gift of the Holy Spirit. This Luke understands as being necessary, for clearly Jesus ascended has in a direct sense of contact, been taken from them. The direct divine dwelling now becomes the Spirit's presence, until Jesus' return again in the parousia. (Acts 1:11) Again, in this giving of the Spirit by Jesus, there is a parallel with the Elijah cycle in that Elijah gives his share of the spirit to Elisha. This giving of the Spirit as the eternal presence differs from Matthew's gospel where the eternal presence will be Jesus himself. (Matt 28:20) The power of the Spirit, Luke has poured on the disciples ten days after the ascension at Pentecost (therefore 50 days after Easter, hence the term Pentecost). Luke strongly understands the community of Jesus' followers as being the community in the power of the Spirit.

Both ascension and Pentecost are thus creations of Luke. They are a means of allowing the physically resurrected Christ to finally ascend to the sphere of the divine, while also guaranteeing ongoing divine presence in the interim between that ascension and the parousia.

Thus empowered the disciples are to be witnesses beginning from Jerusalem, totally now understood as the resurrection location, to 'Judea and Samaria and to the end of the earth.' (Acts 1:8) Galilee is now so relegated to not even being mentioned! To confirm that the resurrection and ascension are all part of one movement, we have the same two angels present at the tomb now ask of the disciples, 'why do you stand looking into heaven?' Even further, this resurrection/ascension cycle is all part of a wider cycle of resurrection, ascension and parousia, whereby 'this Jesus, who was taken up from you into heaven, will come in the same way as you saw him go into heaven.' (Acts 1:11) That Jesus is Messiah is shown by resurrection and ascension and that he shall come again at the eschaton, to bring the fullness of the God's reign. In the interim the community of his followers, empowered by the Holy Spirit, will testify to the veracity of that reign by living lives reflecting its values. Central to that community will be the Apostles, now re-constituted as twelve, following the betrayal by Judas, with the addition

Matthias, chosen by the drawing of lots. (Acts 1: 16-26) As part of this Peter is rehabilitated following his failure at the time of Jesus' arrest. (Acts 1: 15-20, Luke 23:54-62) The story of the spread of this community of Jesus is then told in the rest of this book.[9]

The Lucan account in Acts of the giving of the Holy Spirit at Pentecost is yet another example of midrash, the story drawing from several places in the Hebrew scriptures. First, the breathing of spirit giving new life is drawn from Ezekiel 37, where 'the Spirit of the Lord' breathes life into dry bones that they may live; second, it draws on the image of Elijah calling down fire from heaven in the contest on Mount Carmel, (1 Kgs 18:20-38) and finally it reverses the story of Babel. (Gen 11:1-9) In that Genesis story human pride had led to the confusion of languages (the story representing as such a classic case of myth as explication), while here in the Holy Spirit, the gift of God, people find a unity seen in their being able to hear and understand in their own tongues the good news of Christ. (Acts 2: 1-12) Luke is informing us that, while human hubris divides, the graceful gift of the divine, the Spirit unites, yet does so without squashing the diversity of language, and, we may presume, culture.

John, our fourth gospel, represented a distinct tradition within the early church, and as such bears little similarity to those others we call the synoptic gospels. The Johannine tradition finds expression not only in the gospel, but also in the epistles bearing his name as well as the Book of Revelation. Our other gospels, on the other hand, are Petrine with Mark claiming Peter's authority, and Matthew and Luke drawing on Mark. Here in this gospel however, John, called 'the beloved disciple', is elevated to a position of superiority over Peter. This tradition acts almost like a sideline tradition to that which is central, the Petrine. Even today the lectionary of the church is spread over a three year period, a year being given to each

---

[9] The Book of Acts only picks up some of the spread of the church. It is centered both on the mission and theology of Paul and Peter, who despite their differences, are most prominent. Clearly there were divisions in the early church, as shown even in this book. (Acts 15) Other church traditions existed, including that of the original church centered in Jerusalem under James, the Johannine church, and that founded by the Thomas tradition, which reached as far as India, a few decades after the time of Jesus. The Acts tradition concentrates on the church moving from Jerusalem, the center of the nation, to Rome, the center of the empire, the location of the martyrdom of both Peter and Paul.

of the Petrine gospels, the synoptics, while John, not receiving its own separate year, is only interspersed throughout the other years.

John's gospel is radically different to the other three gospels as even a cursory reading will show. Of particular note, are two very important differences. First, this gospel is marked by what biblical scholars call a 'realized eschatology,' this meaning that the future climatic endpoint, the eschaton, has already found expression in Christ. Thus, John has Jesus say, 'the hour is coming and is now here.' (John 5: 25-26) In John's gospel it may be said, we are indeed living in 'the last days,' for in the Christ event that which the synoptic gospels call the 'reign of God,' is already present, the followers of Christ living in the eschatological era. For this reason the Christian community is called to exhibit those marks associated with the reign of God made already present, especially the trait of love, something core to the Johannine writings. The glorious triumph of Christ in the eschaton has been made particularly present in the resurrection of Jesus, but glory doesn't just stop at the resurrection, but rather is understood as the culmination of the whole Christ event, which for John is full of glory.

This brings us to our second major distinguishing feature in this gospel, John's distinctly different understanding of the connection between passion and resurrection. Whereas in the synoptic gospels, the passion is seen as a necessary prelude to the resurrection, in which true glory lies, John's gospel sees the passion, resurrection and ascension, as one movement of Jesus being lifted up. That physical lifting up on the cross becomes the first part of that movement of being lifted up to glory, initially through the resurrection, and then through the ascension. Thus so, in his great prayer on the eve of his crucifixion, Jesus 'lifts up' his eyes and speaks of the 'glory' he is about to undergo. (John 17:1) Given that this was on the eve of the crucifixion, he has that event in mind, understanding it clearly as glory. Once again this draws us to that Johannine emphasis on love, for in such self-sacrifice given on the torturous instrument of the cross, there can be no greater love shown.

The whole of John's Gospel is written from a post-resurrection perspective with the entirety of Jesus' life being therefore understood through this resurrection lens. This climatic event breaks back, informing the telling of the Jesus story in this gospel, as though it has already occurred, the result being that all in John's Gospel have come to a faith understanding, seeing Jesus as the resurrected one, even though in the story itself technically, that event is still future. Thus the synoptic gospel predictions of the Passion are replaced in this gospel with the 'Son of man' sayings, written from a post-resurrection perspective as indications not of suffering but of glory. (John 3:14, 8:28, 12:31-32) The whole of Jesus' life, including his torturous death, is full of glory.

It is this theme of glory which is so prominent in Jesus' long final sermon, (John 13-17) wherein the cross dominates the whole scene. Therefore, immediately after it is said of Judas, "when he had gone out, Jesus said, 'now is the Son of man glorified and in him God is glorified'." (John 13:31) Again, he speaks of that glory being manifested in the terrible events about to happen, 'and now Father, glorify me in your presence with the glory I had with you before the world was made.' (John 17:5)[10] The cross, as found, is the first step of this being lifted to glory.

Given all this, John is very keen to establish a continuity between the pre-Passion Jesus and Christ resurrected. Thus we have Jesus speak on both sides of that great divide of how he 'must return to the Father,' (John 14:12, 28, 16:10, 17, 28, 17:11, cf. 20:17) while also saying before and after,, 'peace be with you,' (John 14:1, 27, 16:23 cf 20:19, 21:26) and finally likewise in his promises of the 'Paraclete' (literally the alongside witnessing one) generally understood as the Holy Spirit, with his breathing this upon them. (John 14:16, 26, 15:26, 16:7 cf 20:22) This desire for continuity gives John, despite being known as 'the spiritual gospel,' a strong emphasis on the physicality of Jesus' resurrection. This serves again to connect the resurrected one with the pre-crucified one. Thus so, after his resurrection can Mary cling to him, (John 20:17) and Thomas be challenged to 'place your finger here, and look at my hands; then stretch out your hand and

---

[10] In John's Gospel Jesus is most highly glorified, his divinity being pre-existent with God from before creation. This contrasts with Mark's understanding of that son-ship being conferred on Jesus at his baptism. (Mark 1:9-11) Matthew (3:13-17) and Luke (3:21-22), while also speaking of the significance of Jesus' baptism, by their introduction of infancy narratives (which disagree with each other on every point), push that conferral of son-ship, and therefore divinity, back to Jesus' birth. It only leaves John to push that divinity as far back as it is possible to do.

put it in my side.' (John 20:25-27) The resurrected Jesus is no spiritual abstraction separate from the earthly, especially the crucified, Jesus.

In the Johannine account of the resurrection, the language moves back and forth seemingly between the primitive tradition of Jesus being directly exalted to heaven, and the developing tradition of his being resurrected to the earth. As noted, scholars increasingly have come to speak of layers in the Johannine tradition, with the movement of the resurrection understanding serving as further evidence of such development. Therefore, we find the earlier understanding of Jesus' resurrection, non-physical in manner and direct to heaven, from which he makes revelatory appearances, being overlaid with a later tradition, making much of the physicality of the resurrection, while placing it to the earth, where he is seen and even touched, in physical form.

Each of the gospels, it should be noted, gives a different timing for the first coming to the tomb. In this gospel, it is Mary Magdalene alone, who goes to the tomb, 'while it is still dark.' (John 20:1) The darkness here reflects the dualism so present in this gospel, dualism being a means by which contrasts are drawn as oppositions: light/dark, true/false, life/death and such. Here, John's purpose is to affirm the resurrection, understood as light, breaking into the utter darkness which it transforms. For this reason, John has the resurrection witnessed while it was still dark, in contrast to the synoptics who have it witnessed when darkness had already lifted. For John it is the 'son,' rather than the sun, which brings the light breaking the night.

On finding the stone rolled back, Mary races to tell 'Simon Peter and the other disciple, the one Jesus loved.' (John 20:2) Interestingly, she believes that the body has been taken. This would seem then to be an early part of the developing tradition, for it comes before the later construction of the story whereby the body could never have been stolen due to a guard being placed at the tomb. (Matt 28:13-15) Simon Peter, who has been given primacy of position previously, is now joined by this other one 'whom Jesus loved,' while 'the eleven' drop into the background. This other one is almost universally identified as John, the Johannine tradition here at work causing Peter to become subject to this one, whom Jesus seemingly loves above the others. Thus so, on arrival at the tomb John seemingly believes without the need to enter, while Peter needs further proof and must therefore, enter and investigate. (John 20:6-7) That Johannine primacy over Peter is again seen in the following chapter, when while fishing back in Galilee, it is John who immediately recognizes the Lord, while Peter must be told. John in that episode also seems ready to meet the Lord, while Peter not so, needs proper attiring. (John 21:7-8) Despite this being the Johannine tradition, therefore with an attendant desire to elevate John as leader, it would appear that the Petrine tradition is simply too well established to have John being the first to enter the tomb and so be the first witness to the resurrection. The tradition has to make do with him being the faster runner, therefore first to arrive at the tomb, and peering in see the grave clothes. He then, following Peter into the tomb, 'saw and believed.' It is possible that initially this beloved one had no need to enter, for he believed in a manner more spiritual, not needing such proof, but later, as the tradition centered on empirical type proof developed, was understood to have need to enter the tomb. This, however, can only be conjecture.

The empty tomb is now so elevated that it becomes a means in itself of compelling belief. We, given details of the manner of the grave clothes, are compelled, like that other disciple, from that evidence, to 'see and believe.' (John 20: 8) That grave-clothes are left behind by the resurrected Jesus, is different from that found in the episode of Lazarus' resurrection. (John 11: 1-44) There, Lazarus is still wearing grave-clothes when he comes from the tomb. Jesus as the resurrected one, never again to die, will have no more need of such clothes, in contrast to Lazarus who will have such need, for he will again need to pass through the portal of death.

Mary Magdalene, though she has been the first to witness the tomb opened, has not been allowed to be the first into the tomb in this gospel, her role diminished to that of being the one who will fetch the men, who will act as the first real witnesses to the resurrection. Those men, however, having witnessed such, rather anti-climatically and strangely, 'went back to their homes,' (John 20: 10) whereas Mary Magdalene becomes the first to preach the resurrection, (John 20:18) ironically to the still unbelieving apostles. Her witness seemingly, has little effect on the apostles, for we find immediately following written, 'on the evening of that day, the first day of the week, the doors being shut where the disciples were, for fear of the Jews.' (John 20:19) Still timid, the disciples, unlike Mary, are clearly not ready to make such a step to preaching. Again, we catch a glimpse of the important role women played in the resurrection testimony, and no doubt because of such, in the most primitive layer of the church.

We now, however, return to the no doubt older, more authentic tradition, of the women being the first witnesses. Though, 'she stooped to look into the tomb' Mary sees not the grave clothes as evidence, but rather is given testimony by two angels. The low key appearance of the angels probably again indicates an early stage in the developing resurrection tradition which, as with all good stories, gets more and more spectacular as time marches. Initially she sees two angels in white who ask, 'woman, why are you weeping' (John 20:13)? She reports what she believes has happened – the body of Jesus has been stolen. As said, this is an indicator of an early stage of the tradition, before the idea of guards being placed at the tomb to preclude such. In this gospel, Magdalene replaces Matthew's 'chief priests' as believing/creating the story that the body has been stolen. (cf Matthew 27:62-66)

Following her informing the angels of her conclusion of grave-robbing, Mary then hears another voice with the exact same question as to her reason for weeping. Turning, she believes she is talking to the gardener. Of course this 'gardener' is none other than Jesus himself. The same question repeated has turned the appearance of the angels, the angelophony, into the appearance of the divine, a theophany. His calling her by name makes it clear to her just who he is, and replying 'rabboni' or teacher, strangely a not high estimation of the one already shown to be divine in this gospel, she seeks to grasp him. In so doing, Mary in this gospel acts like the three women of Matthew's Gospel, who upon seeing the risen, not yet ascended Jesus in the garden, likewise try to grasp him. (John 20: 17 cf Matt 28:9) Clearly, this grasping may not just be limited to physical grasping, but includes rather the metaphysical grasping or holding on to old concepts – that Jesus is merely 'rabboni' or teacher, but now no longer, both Matthew and John wish us to know, can Jesus be merely grasped by such categories, having become far more. Jesus' response is to use language supporting the idea that he needs to be resurrected or exalted directly to glory, rather than resuscitated to the earth, 'Do not hold me, for I have not yet ascended to the Father.' (John:20:17)

It is very telling at this point that although they have witnessed those things later thought to be the greatest evidence of resurrection – the empty tomb, with stone rolled back, and the folded grave-clothes – such has not elicited any belief from the disciples, who as said, anti-climatically, 'go back to their homes.' Belief rather arises out of what is clearly the older rapture revelatory tradition, associated with Magdalene, the two angels dressed in white and the 'gardener,' actually Jesus!

In passing, it is interesting that Mary has come to make claim for the body of Jesus. Under Jewish law this was the role of the nearest kin. Is there a suggestion that Jesus may have been married to Mary Magdalene? This is not as shocking or outrageous as it sounds, for it was expected of rabbis, and she has just called him thus, that they be married. The idea of religious chastity was very rare, the best known example being some of the Essenes, particularly those at Qumran, the writers and keepers of the Dead Sea Scrolls. If indeed Mary had been married to Jesus, this would serve as a very strong motivation for an increasingly patriarchal church to denigrate her name. In the apocryphal Gospel of Philip it is said that Jesus kissed Mary Magdalene 'often on the mouth.' When the disciples ask why Jesus loves her more than they, he puts the ball back into their court responding, 'why do I not love you like her?' Clearly Jesus is charging them to move to that level of discipleship which Mary exhibits.[11] That this is a late developing part of the tradition ironically makes it in this particular case all the stronger, for by the time of the writing of the Gospel of Philip, the patriarchal structure of the church was clearly well developed. In all of the Johannine resurrection narrative found in this chapter, there are many clues to the prominent position Mary Magdalene held in the primitive church. She is the first to discover the empty tomb, is the one who comes to make claim of his body, while also being the one who receives the first apparition from Jesus, inspiring her to be the first believer and preacher of the gospel. Her name would, however, become besmirched in a most derogatory way so that she ends up, completely contrary to any historical reality, being identified in the Christian tradition as a prostitute. There could obviously be no better way for a patriarchal church to take her down from her perch, and it was very successful. Ask most people, even those who overtly identify as Christians,

---

[11] The dating for the Gospel of Philip is variously given as being between 180-250 CE.

to say something about Mary Magdalene today, that she was a prostitute will just be assumed.[12]

It is appropriate here, while examining the fourth and final gospel, to make an excursus on the central role of women in the testimony of the resurrection across all the gospels. When so doing, we find they are the ones most faithful to Jesus during the time when he is 'in extremis' on the cross, tend the tomb, are the first recipients of the resurrection message, and first to proclaim that message. It is remarkable that the gospels each note this central role, having women give testimony, something which ran entirely contrary to both the contemporary Jewish tradition, and what would develop as the Christian tradition. An example of the context is a near contemporary, the historian Josephus, who expanding on the tradition given concerning witnesses in Deuteronomy 17:6 and 19:15, has Moses prohibit women as witnesses, 'because of their levity and rashness of their sex.' (Ant IV, P.15 [219]) Given this depreciation of women, it seems that there must certainly be a historical kernel to the women being the most faithful supporters of Jesus in his most desperate time, while also being the first resurrection witnesses. It is not the sort of stuff that would be made up! Given the patriarchal tradition, however, it does not take long for that prominent role to begin to be devalued. We perhaps see that happening as early as Mark's gospel, where the women's fear causes them to flee, therefore failing to carry out the task appointed to them. While Matthew has the women, contrary to Mark, carry out the commission given, has them as the first recipients of the resurrection, and again first to offer worship while the men are still full of

---

[12] The method of darkening Mary Magdalene's name is quite ingenious. First she is identified with the Mary of Bethany who anoints Jesus' feet with pure nard, (John 12:1-3) and from that act is linked to another unnamed 'sinful' woman, who washes Jesus' feet and dries them with her hair, while also kissing them. This woman is named as a 'woman of the city' and her many sins are even noted by Jesus. (Luke 7:36-50) It is speculated that because she is 'a sinner,' and that there is a sensuality linked with this action, that she was therefore a prostitute, although that is never stated. Thus, this 'prostitute' anointing the feet of Jesus is linked with Mary of Bethany, who carries out like action, who in turn by sharing the name Mary is linked with Mary Magdalene. This enabled Mary Magdalene to be turned into a prostitute, which in popular imagination she has become. Though Mary Magdalene is mentioned in all four gospels she is never linked with prostitution. The idea of Mary Magdalene being a former prostitute or loose woman dates to Pope Gregory 1 (Gregory the Great) in an influential homily c. 591 CE.

doubt, (Matt 28:17) it will not be them, but rather the men, who will go to Galilee, where Jesus makes his last climatic appearance, commissioning them, not the women, to carry the gospel to the whole world. It would seem in Matthew's Gospel that the appearance to the women has been reduced to being only an anticipation of the central revelation made to the men. In Luke's Gospel, following the narrative of Mark, it is the women who follow Jesus' body to the tomb, prepare spices for his anointing and on return to the tomb finding the stone rolled back are first to hear of the necessity of his death and resurrection, at a time when the apostles dismiss it. (Luke 24:11) Further, numerous scholars suggest that Cleopas' companion on the Emmaus road being un-named, is a female, probably his wife. When the two sojourners return to Jerusalem to relate their experience we are told that they meet with 'the eleven gathered together, and those who were with them.' (Luke 24:33) It is probable that, 'those who were with them' include women. In Acts, following the ascension, we find the disciples who enter the 'upper room' to include named men, who are also joined by 'the women and Mary, the mother of Jesus.' (Acts 1:12-14) Yet, despite all this it is the men, both in Luke's Gospel and its sequel in Acts, who will be credited with carrying the message forward, with their testimony, rather than that of the women, which is believed. Finally, turning to John's Gospel, we again have found women playing a prominent part in the resurrection testimony. This should hardly surprise us, for right through this gospel women have played an important part – the Samaritan woman, (John 4: 7-26) Mary and Martha, Mary, the mother of Jesus and Mary Magdalene. We have just explored how the last named, is central to the Johannine resurrection account.

Yet despite all the prominence of the women, each gospel, with the exception of Mark, who suddenly cuts his gospel after the revelation to the women, asserts male authority and leadership by propelling the story to its 'proper' conclusion, the appearing to, and commissioning by Jesus, of an all-male group. As Judith Lieu says, 'the tradition (of the women's initial witness) was too resilient to be effaced, but it could be confined; restrained and retained so that the women have a voice, but a voice which declares its own limitations.'[13] (29) The truth of the matter, so profoundly known that it could not be erased but rather only re-directed, is that women's testimony

---

[13] Judith Lieu, The Women's Resurrection Testimony in Essays in honour of Leslie Houlden, eds Stephen Barton and Graham Stanton. SPCK, London, 1994: 42

was at the very core of the resurrection witness! When we use, what the feminist biblical scholar Elisabeth Schussler Fiorenza calls, 'a hermeneutic of suspicion,' the truth is clearly seen, not only between the lines of the text, but often surviving even in the text itself.

On returning to our Johannine narrative, following Mary's recounting to the disciples of these things she had witnessed, the risen Christ that evening, makes a sudden rapturous appearance to the disciples, that being necessary as the disciples have not believed the womens' testimony. As established, this type of sudden rapture is indicative of the older layer of tradition. Yet in the midst of this rapturous appearance, there seems to be overwhelming concern by John to show that this risen Christ is indeed the same as the crucified Jesus. There is then an emphasis on the physicality, whereby he shows them, 'his hands and his side.' (John 20: 20) It would appear in this account we have a mixture of the earlier rapturous revelatory resurrection tradition, along with that later tradition built around the physicality of the risen Jesus. As noted, in the evolving Johannine tradition this newer tradition, emphasizing the physicality of the resurrected Jesus, is on a numerous occasions placed on top of that emphasizing the non-physicality of the one, revealed from the heavens to which he has directly ascended, as rapturous vision.

In this appearance, Jesus greets the disciples, that greeting repeated three times – 'Peace be with you,' the same given before the crucifixion to the disciples. (John 14:27) Those words, given previously just prior to Jesus departing from them into his suffering death, now are given again, just as he is about to depart, but this time into glory. This links the whole movement of Jesus to glory – crucifixion, resurrection and ascension – but also establishes the continuity between the pre-crucifixion Jesus and the resurrected one, that clearly being cemented when he shows them his crucifixion wounds. Jesus then breathes the Holy Spirit upon them. As we have found, unlike the Lucan tradition found in Acts, which became normative for the church, wherein the Spirit is not received until 50 days after the resurrection at Pentecost, John has Jesus breathe the Holy Spirit immediately following the resurrection.

'One of the twelve,' Thomas, has not been with the others in these appearances, and in this gospel becomes the figure of doubt. Again this is contrary to the synoptics, where Peter has played that role. By the time of John's final writing, Peter perhaps has become so elevated in the early church that he cannot be the figure of doubt. Perhaps though there may be other reasons for the Johannine tradition identifying Thomas with the figure of doubt. The Thomas tradition was influential within the early church, manifesting itself in the Thomas gospel, as well as the strong tradition of Thomas traveling to India, leading to the establishment of the Mar Thoma Church. The Thomas gospel, as we know, was not accepted by the church as a canonical gospel. This may have been because of its association with Gnosticism, the gospel after-all being found as part of the collection of 'Gnostic Gospels' at Nag Hammadi, Egypt, in 1945. John with his use of contrasting dualist categories, especially light and dark, could have himself been easily identified with the Gnostics, and perhaps in seeking to distance himself from the Thomas tradition, he does so by diminishing Thomas, making him thus this figure of doubt in his gospel.

This line of thought is strengthened when we realize that Thomas is only partially rehabilitated upon Jesus again appearing to the disciples. Strangely, given the compression of the events thus far into one day, we need to wait another eight days for that re-appearance. Then, although the physical proof that Thomas demanded of Jesus' resurrection is on offer, he does not need avail himself of it. His response, 'my Lord and my God,' becomes the high point of understanding among the disciples as to just whom Jesus is, and represents the final response to Jesus in this gospel, putting aside the later appendix, (chapter 21) to which we will turn in a moment. It is clearly meant to be the response of those reading the gospel. Jesus continues however, in a rather disparaging manner, inquiring of Thomas, 'Have you believed because you have seen me?' before adding, 'Blessed are those who have not seen and yet believe.' (John 20:29) These words are directed to those reading John's gospel, right down through the ages within the church, who will believe despite having not physically seen Jesus. These words of Jesus to Thomas, along with the rest of this episode, are intended to represent a disparaging view of those needing the physicality of the resurrection, so to prove it in some manner. As such I understand these words as a protest from within the Johannine tradition of the increasing dominance of the views emphasizing the physicality of the resurrection.

It is interesting to note how John in this chapter, has clearly shown the lack of faith in those who sensually experience the resurrection, despite him having presented to us a Jesus, who during his lifetime spoke of it in a very clear manner. We have seen how the two disciples, Simon Peter and 'the other disciple,' clearly meant to be John, only partially believe when they see the physical evidence of the empty tomb and the manner of how the grave-clothes are left, (John 20:8-9) despite John having Jesus clearly speak of his resurrection, and the Scriptural evidence for it in the body of his gospel, while Mary weeps believing the body to have been taken when she ought, for same reason, to have known that he had risen, something which she still needs to be informed of by the two angels. (John 20:11) The disciples, despite the resurrection, merely go 'back to their homes,' and are later still shown to be living in fear behind locked doors, (John 20:19) while Thomas fails to believe in the resurrection even though informed by 'the other disciples.' (John 20:25) This unbelief is then trumped by Thomas' great statement of faith, 'my Lord and my God' (John 20:28) which, as we have seen, only wins muted approval from Jesus. The ability of physical evidence to compel belief seems to be held in low regard by John.

The chapter then concludes in summary form by saying that Jesus did many other 'signs,' which are not written in this book. In using the word 'sign' John is exhibiting his different understanding of the miracles worked by Jesus. The miracles in John's understanding aren't marvels in themselves upon which one should be fixated, but rather as signs serving to point to deeper realities. In constructing his gospel John has seven of these great signs, each followed by a long discourse, given by Jesus, examining those deeper things to which the miracles as signs point. This is distinct from the synoptics, where the miracles understood as 'wonders' and 'powers,' represent in themselves evidence for Jesus' status.

Finally John gives reason for the writing of his book, and with this intention there is great debate. That debate centers on the verb 'believe.' The tense used determines whether the translation should be, 'might come to believe' or 'might continue to believe.' There is strong textual evidence for both with the question being raised then, whether the gospel is written with an evangelistic purpose as the first translation would have, or as a means of strengthening existing belief.[14] It of course can be used for both, and perhaps the ambiguity is intentional.

In examining this chapter, the first of two resurrection accounts in this gospel, we have found evidence for the layering of the tradition, the new upon the old. The earlier tradition is represented by such things as the appearance of the angels, Magdalene's not recognizing Jesus' resurrected form until it is revealed to her by his speaking her name, and also his response instructing her not to hold him. Further evidence for that earlier tradition is found in how Jesus magically manifests himself twice to the disciples behind closed doors. These all pick up the earlier rapture or revelatory tradition of the resurrection, along with its incorporeal nature. In the later tradition, the resurrection is objectified by such things as the empty tomb with stone rolled away, the state of the grave-clothes, and Jesus twice offering of physical proof. Here, the resurrection is corporeal and has the earth as its initial location.

Let us turn to what is now the last chapter in John's Gospel, chapter 21. Clearly, this is a later addition, for if chapter 21 was part of the original gospel why does chapter 20 draw so clearly to what is obviously meant to be the conclusion of the gospel? As such, the Johannine Gospel would read better without it, and we may ask just what is added to the gospel by its presence. It clearly comes, however, sufficiently early in the Johannine tradition for it to be accepted as a legitimate part of the gospel, no manuscript been found not containing it as a part of the gospel. More evidence of it being distinct is found in its vocabulary and grammar, these being in this chapter somewhat different from the rest of the gospel. Further, the writer of this chapter speaks of 'the beloved disciple' in the third person rather than, as in the rest of the gospel, the first person. (John 21:20-23) Perhaps the motivation for this chapter is that increasing numbers of witnesses to both

---

[14] The question revolves around strong competing textual evidence. An aorist subjunctive of the Greek verb *'pisteuo'* 'to believe' allows for a translation of, 'might come to believe,' which implies John addressing an unbelieving audience, his gospel having then an evangelistic purpose. On the other hand, the present tense normally means 'might continue believe,' implying John addressing a believing audience, the purpose of his gospel being then to encourage and edify existing believers. The difference revolves around one letter, iota or i. Of course the gospel lends itself to being used both ways.

Jesus' life and resurrection are dying, for there is clearly a great concern for such aging and dying in this chapter. (John 21:18-23)

The chapter consists of Jesus' appearance to the disciples while they were fishing on the Sea of Tiberias (Lake Galilee), the sharing of the meal on the beach, and a section meant to show the primacy of John over Peter. The first two of these episodes are marked, as in Luke's Emmaus story, by those seeing Jesus not being able to easily recognize him, while again, as in the Emmaus story, there are Eucharistic connections linked to the sea side meal. The section affirming John's primacy involves a three-fold restoration of Peter, that being another sign of Johannine primacy, for John has no need of such, this also being present in Jesus' harsh reply to Peter's questioning concerning John's fate, 'what is that to you?' (John 21:22) Peter, in relation to John, by Jesus' answer, is being very clearly put in his place.

There are several further clues that within this chapter which show us that it is an addition. This chapter commences with the appearance of Jesus at the Sea of Tiberias and consequent meal, which we are told was the 'third time that Jesus was revealed to the disciples after he was raised from the dead,' (John 21:14) yet the previous chapter has him already revealed three times, to Magdalene, the disciples without Thomas, and then the disciples with Thomas. Further, if the disciples have grasped anything of the significance of Jesus' resurrection, and have received the Holy Spirit, as stated in chapter 20, it seems strange that they have merely returned to their old occupation. Again, if we are to understand that Jesus has, as claimed in the previous chapter, been revealed at all, it seems strange here, that despite previous appearances, the disciples on the boat 'did not know that it was Jesus,' (John 21:4) despite being 'not far from the land,' (John 21:8) even following his speaking to them. Once they do apprehend just who he is, their daring not to ask him as to his identity, 'for they knew it was the Lord,' (John 21:12) again sounds much more like a first meeting than a third or even fourth meeting. The final clue is that Peter is not rehabilitated until here. As the chief apostle in the early church there clearly is a need for that, the tradition of his denial seemingly well known. This chapter is largely concerned for that rehabilitation. As we have seen, the Johannine tradition represents a stream independent from the main Petrine tradition represented in the other gospels. If this chapter is a later addition, Peter's increasing elevation in the mainline tradition necessitates that he find redemption in this Johannine tradition, this probably being the main reason for its addition.[15]

On first turning to this chapter we are immediately struck by the change of locale. Indeed it is pointed out to us. 'After this Jesus revealed himself again to the disciples by the Sea of Tiberius' (Galilee). (John 21:1) We are back at the older Galilee resurrection tradition, at odds with the previous chapter with its Jerusalem tradition. The word 'revealed' of Jesus' resurrection is used in a manner peculiar to this chapter. When used elsewhere in the gospel it speaks of a manifestation or revelation, non-objective in manner, to be seen only through the right eyes. (John 3:21, 7:4, 9:3, 17:6) Thus, it would appear the resurrection appearance of Jesus here in Galilee is of the older rapture or revelatory manner. Seemingly, in the Johannine tradition, there are then two separate traditions, one centered in Galilee, the other in Jerusalem.

The initial story in this chapter has the disciples, after an unsuccessful night of fishing, being told by this 'stranger' to cast their nets to the right hand side of the boat, whereupon doing so, they pull in a miraculously extraordinary catch of fish. The catch is so large that they are unable to draw it in, the quantity of fish clearly being indicative of the massive task with which the disciples will be presented in proclaiming the gospel. As yet they have not recognized Jesus and without him, John wants us to know, the task of pulling in the catch is beyond them. (John 21:6) Following the recognition of Jesus however, they are now able to haul in the net full of fish. (John 21:8) The story seems to be drawing on material found also in Luke's Gospel. There, the story of the miraculous catch of fish represents the calling of Peter, who breaks down before Jesus, early in Jesus' ministry,

---

[15] That rehabilitation is done with a subtlety absent from the English translations. Greek has a number of words of varying intensity and meaning for love. Thus, when Peter is asked the first time, he is being asked "do you 'agape' (total non-ego centered love) me more than these?" replies "yes Lord, you know that I 'phileo' (like you as a friend) you." On the second occasion he is asked again, "do you 'agape' me?" with no comparison being made to others this time. Again, he responds using 'phileo.' On the third occasion Jesus lowers the bar asking "do you 'phileo' me?" Peter understands what is happening and is 'grieved' and responds, "you know that I 'phileo' you." The three fold recommissioning where Peter is instructed to 'feed my lambs/sheep,' parallels the three fold failure of his denial of Jesus before the crucifixion.

(Luke 5:1-11) while here the miraculous catch is translated to being a post-resurrection episode, associated with Peter's rehabilitation and being called again, following his failure at the time of Jesus trial. When indirectly reminded of that he breaks down before Jesus, as he had broken down in the Lucan story (John 21:17).

The chapter concludes with the rehabilitation of Peter, though in a manner which still leaves evident his failure, and therefore subservience to John. To match his thrice-said denial at Jesus' trial (John 18:15-18) Peter is three times given opportunity to express his love of Jesus. (John 21:15-17) Peter is judged harshly here because of that denial, though we should remember this is from within the Johannine tradition. Then after being told of how he would die, 'hands outstretched,' this surely being from the tradition following Peter's crucifixion, Peter rehabilitated is charged, 'follow me.' Where before, Peter cannot follow Jesus to his crucifixion, thrice denying him, we are, following his thrice-fold rehabilitation, told that this following is precisely what he will do, or more accurately has already done, even to death, by the time of the writing of this account.

Peter then turns and sees 'following them the disciple whom Jesus loved.' (John 21: 20) Again, we find Johannine primacy, for while Peter has been charged to start following Jesus, it is clear that this disciple has already committed himself to such a course of following. There follows a hint of jealousy from Peter concerning this figure, meaning that Jesus must again adjure him, 'follow me.' Obviously Peter's jealousy has not been helped by Jesus' ambiguous words concerning this disciple remaining until he comes. So elevated is this other disciple, whom we know is John, that, 'a saying spread around the believers that this disciple was not to die.' (John 21: 23) We know that this is John because he (of course more accurately the Johannine tradition) confesses to writing the account, (John 21:24) concluding as at the end of chapter 20, that this is only a partial account of, the many other things which Jesus did, which if recorded could not be contained in all 'the books which could be written.'

What are we to make of our examination of the five very distinct resurrection accounts found in Paul, Mark, Matthew, Luke and John? In brief, we have seen two over-arching themes, first of how over time there is a movement from a non-corporeal resurrection made direct to the heavens, from where Jesus is revealed to those upon the earth in a revelatory rapturous manner, to one where he is resurrected directly back to the earth physically, in which manner he reveals himself to those who see him. This change is associated with an ever stronger desire to both, make sense of an essentially ineffable experience, also to counter a type of spiritualized resurrection as the Gnostics would have, and finally make some sense of it, perhaps even give some type of proof. This last aspect, along with the nature of story being more easily remembered, are means also which enable the resurrection to be communicated.

Second, we have seen how the location for the resurrection also moves from Galilee to Jerusalem. This again is expected, for the early followers of Jesus increasingly desire to place their story at the heart of their tradition, rather than having it marginalized in the 'back woods' of Galilee. The Jesus story they claim has a universal significance, Jerusalem being a starting point, from where it will be carried over the whole world.

I wish now to turn to those things which I view as giving the evidence for this thing called resurrection, something which by its very essence beyond our human experience, must remain elusive.

Chapter Six

The deeper evidence

I want now to commence our examination of what I understand serves as the deeper evidence for the resurrection, by first dealing with those things usually held as being evidence of it. These are those things usually adduced as proof – the empty grave, the manner in which the grave-clothes are left, the appearances of Jesus on numerous occasions in a manner which is meant to show that they were physical in manner, in that Jesus shares in eating, or offers exploration of his bodily wounds. A careful reading of these, however, will see that none of them compel belief in those witnessing, and they are not used by any of the gospel writers as means of compelling faith. Indeed, in each gospel, instead of compelling faith, they serve rather to sow confusion and fear. This need not unduly concern us, for if we remain in the sphere of history for proof of the resurrection we are short-changed. Of this type of evidence for the resurrection Robert Morgan concludes, 'Where the Gospel record makes an historical claim, we may accept it, be skeptical, or remain agnostic. Our judgments may be influenced by our metaphysical beliefs, but these are unlikely to be reshaped by such weak historical evidence as the gospels provide. It is therefore liberating to learn that God's raising Jesus is not an historical event, whatever its historical effects, and that the grounds for our believing are not the evidence of Easter Sunday (or thereabouts), even if these now obscure events played a role in establishing the faith of the first disciples.'[1] I intend to show there are apologetic and theological, rather than historical, reasons for the description of resurrection as being bodily or en-fleshed.

It is crucially important to reiterate that those accounts within the gospel tradition which are commonly later, and still indeed today, taken as being attempts to prove the resurrection, are never understood that way within those documents. Once we get past our preconceived ideas that this was what the gospel writers were intending to do, their actual intention

---

[1] Robert Morgan, Flesh is Precious: The Significance of Luke 24:36-43 in Essays in honour of Leslie Houlden, eds Stephen Barton and Graham Stanton. Society for the Propagation of Christian Knowledge, London, 1994: 12

becomes very clear. Let us now turn to examine how with fear and non-comprehension each so-called 'proof' of resurrection, is met by those who experience it in our canonical gospels.

On doing so, we immediately find that from the earliest episode, the empty tomb in Mark's Gospel, we have the women described as, 'fleeing from the tomb, for trembling and astonishment had come upon them: and they said nothing to anyone, for they were afraid.' (Mark 16:8) Rather than being convinced by the appearance of the young man, clearly meant to be understood as an angelic figure, to go and tell 'the disciples and Peter,' that Christ has risen, giving as evidence the empty grave, the women simply respond in fear and seeming confusion. Even in the added addendum to Mark's Gospel that disbelief continues with the apostles dismissing Mary Magdalene's testimony, (Mark 16:11) while even a direct appearance of the risen Christ to two of the apostles fails to elicit belief. (Mark16:12-13) In the Markan addendum Jesus has to actually upbraid the apostles, 'for their unbelief and hardness of heart, because they had not believed those who saw him after he had risen.' (Mark 16:14)

In Matthew's heightened account of the empty tomb the women are again 'afraid,' (Matt 28:5) and while they respond with 'joy' concerning the now clearly denoted angel, they still depart with fear. (Matt 28:8) Fear is the dominant feeling, for when Jesus appears to them, he must admonish them, 'Do not be afraid.' (Matt 28:10) Here, we interestingly find one of those physical things supposedly meant to elicit faith present, for we read, 'and they came and took hold of his feet and worshipped him.' (Matt 28:9) Despite this physicality present here, it is clear that it takes more than the mere miraculous physical presence, for the disciples to move beyond fear. Clearly the style of 'worship' being spoken here seems to have more to do with being 'awestruck,' rather than being an empowering experience of resurrection. Despite all this 'proof' which is supposedly meant to convince concerning the resurrection, 'doubt' is present to the very end of Matthew's gospel, where we read of the apostles, that while some 'worshiped him,' others 'doubted.' (Matt 28:17) Clearly proof cannot compel belief in the resurrection. Its truth must lie deeper than that. Indeed, the only time following his resurrection that the disciples truly express their belief in Matthew's Gospel is in the very last verses, (Matthew 28: 16-20) when they ascend a mountain where Jesus meets them. It is clearly implied that he has not ascended the mountain with them, but rather has descended from on high in the more primitive rapturous or revelatory appearance.

In Luke's Gospel we still have the first witnesses, the women, 'perplexed' and 'frightened.' (Luke 24:4-5) Here, even though the angelic figures seemingly convince the women, Mary Magdalene, Johanna and Mary, here called the 'mother of James,' of the resurrection, the story this still does not elicit belief among the apostles, who dismiss the report as an 'idle tale' which they clearly associate with women. (Luke 24:11) Thus, we find, probably quite deliberately, the word opposite to belief, 'disbelief' used in reference to the apostles. Many manuscripts include a verse missing in the 'received text' which again reinforces how the physical 'proofs' of the resurrection fail to elicit belief.[2] The missing verse says, following the report of the women, 'But Peter rose and ran to the tomb; stooping and looking in, he saw the linen cloths by themselves; and he went home wondering at what had happened.' (Luke 24:12) Moving on to the next episode in this gospel, the Emmaus story, we find yet again, that it is not the empty tomb, nor visions of angels, which causes belief, such being very clear from the story, (Luke 24:22- 24) but rather the deeper things which the person journeying with them, Jesus, whom they cannot recognize, must explain to them, from 'what the prophets had spoken.' (Luke 24:25) The 'stranger' begins that explanation by linking the 'glory' of the Christ with the need for him to 'suffer these things.' (Luke 24:26) The glory of the transformed resurrected person, Jesus, unrecognizable to the sojourners, is being essentially linked to the 'suffering body.' The goal of Luke is not to prove the resurrection by presenting the resurrected body as evidence, but rather to make clear a theological point, that the resurrected one is in bodily form, the same bodily form which endured suffering. The continuity between the resurrected Christ and the crucified Jesus is drawn by use of the continuity of body. Embodiment is not used to prove resurrection, but rather to show the nature of that resurrection. This informs the rest of this episode where the stranger is seemingly in need of a meal and a bed for the night. (Luke 24:28-31) Embodiment is there also

---

[2] The received text represents that text arrived at by scholars for which they believe there is the greatest textual evidence among the plethora of manuscripts discovered. It nowhere exists in antiquity as an actual text but is rather an accumulation of all the different texts and manuscript evidence for them, drawn up by scholars. Given that the Christian Scriptures are written in koine (common) Greek it of course exists in that language drawn up by scholars representing such bodies as the United Bible Society, from where it is translated into contemporary languages

used as a means of establishing how one should act to care for another's bodily needs for such things as food and lodging. By such caring one grasps and appropriates the resurrection. Embodiment again serves to illustrate the means of understanding resurrection rather than representing proof.

Later, Jesus again appears to the gathered apostles, as they were receiving the report from those who had been on the road, where we also hear of a report of an appearance to Simon. Here, 'Jesus himself stood among them.' (Luke 24:36) Such an appearance, again however, does not bring forth faith, but rather results in their being 'frightened.'

We can conclude then that for Luke, the main purpose of the supposed resurrection proofs is that Jesus' presence is drawn as being opposite to a mere spirit presence. Jesus says, 'See my hands and my feet, that it is I myself; handle me, and see; for a spirit does not have flesh and bones as you see I have.' (Luke 24:39-40) Luke again shows the limitation of the physicality of resurrection as proof when he speaks of the apostles 'still disbelieving,' necessitating Jesus to eat a piece of fish in their presence. Even then the physicality of the resurrection seemingly does not elicit belief, for even after Jesus eats the fish, no word is said about the apostles now believing. The apostles finally come to belief as a whole in the same manner as did the two on the road to Emmaus, when Jesus 'opened their minds to understand the scriptures.' (Luke 24:45) Again, as in the previous episode, the rising from the dead is linked to the necessity that 'the Christ should suffer.' There clearly needs be established, a continuity between the suffering body and the resurrection physicality. Again, I reiterate, this rather than the physical nature of the resurrection acting as proof for its reality thereby compelling belief, is the purpose of the emphasis on its physical form. Luke's Gospel has been held up as that most affirming the physicality of Jesus' resurrection, it being commonly used in attempts to prove the veracity of the resurrection, by reference to its physicality. However, as we have seen, in Luke, as in the other synoptics, there is no ringing out of the 'Hallelujah Chorus' on any of those occasions when physical manifestations on the resurrection are given. Rather, quite the opposite – confusion, fear, timidity and disbelief.

On turning to John's Gospel, we have everything heightened so that faith in the risen Christ, resurrection faith, stretches back and shapes the whole gospel narrative. Thus, here the empty tomb and the particular manner in which the grave-clothes are left do elicit belief, but that belief is already assumed. (John 20:8) Further, it is to be expected that these things will elicit belief for such is in accord with the Scriptures. (John 20:9)

John's Gospel, as said, is written in several layers of tradition and my belief is that the certainty expressed in the resurrection through such physically evidential signs, represents a later layer of those traditions. An earlier layer of tradition, I surmise, is present in the following story of Mary's (possibly the mother of Jesus or Magdalene) encounter with 'the gardener.' (John 20:11-18) The insertion of the first story of Peter and 'the other disciple' running to the tomb serves largely to take away the prime place of the women as being first witnesses to the resurrection. In that story we find that there is no primacy in the women's discovery for they do not enter the tomb, but rather, only observing from some distance that the stone has been rolled away, assume that someone had taken the body. In the succeeding story, however, it is a woman, Mary, who represents the first to come to faith concerning the resurrection. (John 20:18) Thus, it is the second story with its primacy of the women's witness, which I strongly believe represents the older tradition. What do we find there?

On looking at this second story, we find we are back at that earlier understanding, whereby the physical nature of the resurrection does not have as its goal proof of that event, but rather serves to point to its nature, the event after-all being one in which faith was already present, as being physical in continuity with the broken physical body of Christ. There is no need to prove the resurrection, for it is assumed already present in 'the Scriptures' (meaning of course the Hebrew Scriptures) for those who have eyes to see. The physicality of the resurrection for John is not a means of proof, but rather something by which he links the resurrected Christ to Jesus, particularly the Jesus dying upon the cross. It has a theological, as we would expect with John, reason at its core, rather than one of offering some type of objective proof.

The next story in John's resurrection account is surely deliberately framed by this concern. Jesus suddenly stands among the disciples, though they are hiding behind 'locked doors.' John clearly wishes us to know that this is a type of rapturous revelatory appearance. Jesus then says, 'peace be with you,' a means, as earlier explored, of linking this resurrected one to the one who announces these words on the eve of his execution. Then the story turns very physical with Jesus showing his hands and side, they bearing the marks of his crucifixion. Such is often used by those wishing to prove the physicality of the resurrection. Yet clearly it is the theological agenda of John, whereby he wishes to root this resurrected one into the crucified one, hence the showing of the crucifixion marks, which is predominant here, rather than any idea of using physicality as a means of proving the resurrection. After-all if we are speaking of physicality just how did this one enter the room though the doors were locked? This is reinforced by the disciples' reactions. There is no belief elicited by this 'physical' manifestation, belief rather, only present when he breathes the Holy Spirit upon them. (John 20:22- 23) The story then continues, informing us that one of the disciples, Thomas, was missing from the group, and on receiving their report of Jesus' appearance to them, he proves to be a skeptic, demanding physical proof of being able to explore Jesus' physical wounds. As we earlier explored, when he has the opportunity to explore those wounds, he has no need. John clearly is telling us that it is not physicality which proves the resurrection, but something far more profound. The appearance of Jesus on this occasion is again rapturous, revelatory in nature, John clearly indicating that, by again telling us that 'the doors were shut.' John concludes, reinforcing just what I have been saying, by informing us that Jesus says to John, 'have you believed because you have seen me? Blessed are those who have not seen yet believe.' (John 20: 29) The limitations of physical manifestations of the resurrection could hardly be more strongly expressed!

On turning to the appended chapter to John's Gospel, we again see the limitations of the physical resurrection. Jesus is seen on the beach by the disciples, returned to their old trade, fishing, who however do not recognize him, even when he speaks to them. (John 21:4-8) Recognition comes only when following his command, though to the experienced fishermen it must have seemed illogical. When the disciples follow that command, with an overwhelming result, 'the disciple whom Jesus loved' suddenly realizes, 'it is the Lord.' Recognition of Jesus has not come via physical means as proof, but rather by following his commands. When the rest of the disciples come ashore with a boat loaded with fish, they join Jesus for a meal, he not being dependent on their fish, having some of his own. We read then, 'none of the disciples dared ask, "who are you?" They knew it was the Lord.' (John 21:12). Clearly the recognition of Jesus again is by non-sensual means.

Even though John's whole account of the resurrection is colored by his pre-supposition that it stretches back informing the whole gospel, still the physicality of it, when made present, is not the means of compelling belief. As in the synoptics, perhaps even more so in John's Gospel, the physical nature of the resurrection owes more to theological reason than any objective historicity. This is to be expected for with most, if not all, things in John, there is a strong theological rationale, rather than objective historical interest informing the way the gospel is composed. Let us examine those theological reasons.

John is often said to be the most spiritual of the gospels, but is extremely careful not to present Jesus' resurrection as being in nature spiritual only. John links the whole process of cross, resurrection and ascension together, as all being part of Jesus' being raised to glory, the continuity of the physicality of Jesus being assumed all the way through. This concern to emphasize physicality in the resurrection, and the continuity between the crucified and resurrected one, may have been a reaction, as we have seen, when discussing his darkening of Thomas' reputation, so to clear himself from any charge of Gnostic tendencies. Yet, to be fair to John I understand there to be more to it than that. John is very much the gospel of love, and there can hardly be anything more earthed and present in corporeal form, than love as exhibited in the crucifixion. In such for John is true glory.

We can safely conclude then, that all those physical evidences commonly taken as proofs for the resurrection – the empty tomb, the grave-clothes, the physical, though transformed appearances of Jesus – are clearly not intended by the authors to be some type of evidence which elicits belief, for in the gospel accounts they never do so. This is only to be expected for the gospels are written to communities already believing in the resurrection, with no need therefore for it to be proven. Being thus written to those already believing communities, the physicality of the resurrection is meant both to act as an antidote to the Gnostic ideas which were prevalent, almost pervasive, in the wider cultural milieu, therefore increasingly influencing Christianity, while also communicating a profoundly deep resurrection experience, which could only be effectively communicated by such means. The accounts do not have as their goal the giving of objective history, but that rather have as their main concern theology and apologetics. As such the gospels are not endeavoring to prove resurrection as an empirical fact which compels belief through these physical signs, but rather are using these things in two ways, the first to best communicate a profound transformative experience to which the earliest Christians had been subject, the second, to argue in countering the Gnostics, that the resurrection is not some spiritual thing alone.

Let us turn to the first of these. It seems that as humans we are unable to live by experience alone, or perhaps we are unable to communicate it to succeeding generations with that same intensity with which it struck us. The non-transferable nature of such profound experience means there is therefore a need to objectify or concretize it, both as a means of defense against detractors, who deny the validity of the experience, and also to provide a means of passing it on. There is a need to construct stories in order to communicate, but these stories operate mythologically and metaphorically. The storyline in myth and the symbolic metaphor, are not meant to be taken literally. Rather, it communicates the profound in an attempt to open the reader to the original experience. This is not to denigrate the writings, but rather on the contrary to approach them in the deeper manner, which the original writers intended.

Despite what I have said about the stories not being designed as proofs they do, however, have an interest in stating that the resurrection wasn't just simply concocted, and therefore a lie. Thus the charge by the detractors that the body of Jesus was merely stolen by the believers is, as we have seen, countered by the creation of the story of Roman guards watching the tomb. (Matt 27:62-66, 28:11-15) This story, I feel, is a type of concession to the literal. The opponents of the resurrection are arguing on literal grounds, and so are countered on those grounds. There is no other option here, but the manner in which this story seeks to compel a stance on the veracity of the resurrection, shows it to be clearly different to those others which make up the resurrection accounts.

To those that charge that the resurrection was mere hysterical hallucination, the gospels are concerned to show the risen Christ, raised in physical form, as continuous with the earthly Jesus in his physicality, even showing his crucifixion wounds. (Luke 24:39, 41-43, John 20:20, 27) This concern to refute the hallucinatory only nature of the resurrection is behind all the 'proofs' given in the gospels – the empty tomb, the graveclothes, the stone rolled away, the lying of the temple guards and event the witness of the 'figure in white'/angel. During the second century an opponent of the Christian church, Celsus, charged that if Jesus had really wanted to prove his resurrection, he would have appeared to those who had killed him, so to vindicate himself. His argument however, had already been anticipated in the Scriptures wherein it is claimed that he only revealed himself to those he chose, rather than to all. (John 14:18-22, Acts 10:40-42) This claim that the resurrection is more than just a non-physical hallucinatory thing brings us to the second reason for the construction of the resurrection accounts.

The stories, as seen, have also a theological purpose, in that they are constructed to defend a particular view of the resurrection to the exclusion of others, particularly in how they operate as a defense against Gnosticism. The physicality of the resurrection was at the heart of the church's defense against the various schools of Gnosticism, with their emphasis on the spiritual as being essentially opposed to the physical, the former good, the latter evil. Gnosticism was a dangerous temptation for Christians, especially as they came more under the influence of Hellenist thought. With their disparagement of the physical, Gnostic systems of thought presented a threat to the very essence of the Christian story, which claimed that the divine had taken human form in Jesus. Clearly, where the physicality of Jesus was most at question was in his resurrection, and thus it is here that the gospels strongly assert physicality of this resurrection as means of defense. This explains why the developing tradition so sought to proclaim a doctrine so contrary to usual notions of resurrection in the ancient world. To the amorphous mix of Gnosticism the church sought to speak of the unique place of the historical Jesus in the clearest terms, with therefore a need to take his resurrection out of the realm of subjective experience and historicize it. In order to do that, they en-fleshed it, but clearly never intended this corporeal nature to be taken literally. That intention is, as already shown, quite explicit in how they tell the stories. Thus, so to read the accounts in the gospels and to hold a literal view of Jesus' resurrection in corporeal form would lead to all sorts of conundrums, among them, non-recognition of one intimately known, sudden appearances in locked rooms, and the ascension to the heavens. Rather, the corporeal nature of the resurrection operates as a profound metaphor affirming the continuity of the resurrected one with the pre-crucifixion Jesus, while also affirming the essential goodness of the physical order. The physical nature of resurrection is intended to assert the essential goodness of creation, human and otherwise, against the idea that it needed to be transcended in the realm of the spiritual. That affirmation of the physical was also an affirmation of the incarnation, in that the church charged God had taken human physical form. The resurrected Christ is not one who can be abstracted speculatively from the physical Jesus, as though the goodness of the resurrected spiritual one was due to his having left his physical form behind. The antidote to such a view is found in how the gospels inform us that the two, the crucified Jesus, and the resurrected Christ, are the same as evidenced through the continuity of their en-fleshed nature.

Resurrection clearly is something beyond normal human sensual experience in that it clearly totally transcends it. However, as we have seen, the needs of the infant church, especially in light of its opponents, meant that this institution continually found it necessary to concretize that original ineffable non-quantifiable experience, in order to communicate it and also to defend its nature against Gnostic anti-corporeal understandings. That concretization, as we have observed, would continue past the time of the writing of the Christian Scriptures.

Given that today such literalist readings, rather than providing us with evidence for the veracity of the resurrection, have instead become problematical, it is perhaps providential that we have, as found, some other understandings of the resurrection left to explore. That these are chronologically nearer to the actual event serves to call us to more closely examine them if we are to maintain belief in the resurrection. Put bluntly, what has become Christian orthodoxy concerning the resurrection, is no longer credible in a world 'come of age.' We cannot continue to read the biblical narratives of the resurrection as though they were descriptions of empirical, historical events. This is particularly the case when it comes to those parts of the resurrection story which specify it in a manner as though it were obtainable by proofs.[3]

---

[3] 'Biblical narrative is rarely well interpreted if one understands it as a direct neutral transcript of a prior empirical reality, and such an approach is particularly problematic in the case of the gospel post-resurrection appearances, granted the obvious and well known divergences between them all.' Francis Watson, 'He is not here': Towards a Theology of the Empty Tomb in Resurrection, Essays in honour of Leslie Houlden, 98

If not from such concrete proofs where then can we find evidence then for the resurrection? If such proofs can't be found is resurrection not reduced to being an existential, perhaps mystical experience with no manner of being passed on, only attainable as a deep individual experience? As such is it nothing more than a metaphor for hope, renewal, re-birth, the coming of the spring, chrysalis and such? There is essentially nothing wrong with these, for they are powerful and important metaphors when it comes to resurrection, but clearly the resurrection of Christ in the midst of history, both vindication for the horrendous death he suffered, that being a consequence of all that he stood for, and also as an anticipatory sign for the reign of God, requires something more, I believe, than general metaphor.

I hold we can find that evidence for the resurrection which we need, but having said that we cannot tie it down in any manner that say would represent proof say in a Court of Law. The evidence comes from the resurrection belief in the early church, a belief which goes back in credal form to the most primitive layer of the tradition.

That most primitive layer of the tradition was oral so we cannot be sure just what that was, but that tradition does however very early take written form, not with the gospels, but as we have noted, with the correspondence of Paul. He has as he says, no interest in 'Christ from a human point of view,' (2 Cor 5:16) with his theology being firmly centered on the risen resurrected Christ. Paul is writing his letters just 20-30 years after the claimed event of Jesus' rising from death, and within these letters we find passages which appear to contain even earlier credal statements, liturgical forms or perhaps songs, from a period before that. Some examples shall suffice. The best known is that of Philippians 2:5-11, where of Christ it says, 'He always had the nature of God... of his free will he gave up all he had and took the nature of a servant. He was humble and walked the path of obedience all the way to death – his death on the cross. For this reason God raised him to the highest place above.' Though resurrection is not directly mentioned here, the 'raised him' in particular, but the passage as a whole, is shot through with the assumption of the resurrection. In the chapter in which Paul speaks in most detail of the resurrection he culminates in exultatory language noting, "the saying that is written, 'death is swallowed up in victory. O death where is thy victory? O death where is thy sting'?" (1 Cor 15:55) This sounds like a type of very early liturgical form, perhaps even triumphal song used in the infant church. It may be pointed out that it has connections with Hosea 13:14, though that would not preclude it being re-worked into an early liturgical piece, testifying to the resurrection. Again, to the Corinthians Paul writes, how he had received, therefore from a pre-existing tradition, concerning the resurrection, 'I passed on to you what I received, which is of the greatest importance: that Christ died for our sins, as written in the Scriptures; that he was buried and that he was raised to life three days later as written in the Scriptures.' (1 Cor 15:3-4) Clearly, he understands himself as the recipient of an already existing tradition. From such evidence, we can only but conclude that the resurrection tradition goes back to the very earliest level of the infant church.

That there was, and indeed still is a church established on belief in the resurrection, testifies to its veracity. That there is such a body, the church, built on the worship of Jesus is remarkable, given that his life had actually ended in failure. Everything about which he had preached, had not eventuated. There was no advent of the Kingdom of God, however one understood that. Rome had not been overthrown, Israel was not free, oppression and injustice continued, wealth was still mal-distributed, the wealthy still ruled, and the only 'peace' was that enforced at the end of a Roman spear. The one who had announced the coming of the reversal of all these things, taking his stand against the powers, rather than defeating them, had been taken by those powers, and like any other rebel, been summarily dealt with, Roman 'justice' having him strung up on a cross with other rebels, whom our gospels designate as 'thieves.'[4] There he would endure an unbearable physical agony, caused by the cruelest form of torture the Roman mind could devise.

While he was agonizingly slowly dying, the carrion were no doubt waiting, or perhaps already taking their piece of flesh, the undefended

---

[4] I believe the gospel accounts of appearances before Pilate and the supposed reticence, indeed agony, of that man to pronounce execution upon Jesus, are a clear fabrication. As a peasant insurrectionist, whom Rome executed by the thousands, it is unlikely that Jesus would have merited a trial before the Prefect. It is far more likely that Jesus was simply summarily dealt with without any real trial. The Sanhedrin appearance is even less likely on the eve of Pesach (Passover). A Galilean peasant rebel stirring up trouble at a time of the great nationalist festival of Pesach, when the population of Jerusalem swelled some 10 fold would not be expected to last long.

eyes being prime target. Suffocating as he fell forward from time to time, Jesus would have pushed himself up by his legs, something causing indescribable pain as the nails through the feet, were placed through the heel bone, thus designed to cause the greatest pain and to preclude any merciful quick 'bleeding out' hastening death. All this took place on the main thoroughfare, as warning to any other 'would be rebels' such as those who had most closely followed this man. To make the scene complete the Romans mockingly placed a sign, 'King of the Jews,' written in Greek, Latin and Hebrew above his head, ensuring all would understand that here before you is the fate of any who dare proclaim a kingship and kingdom in opposition to Caesar and Rome. His end in such manner it need hardly be said, was not that envisioned for the Messiah! As Jesus died there was no reign of God, no new era, just the continuation of that which had always been. The one announced as the Messiah, in whom many had placed their hope to bring down the wrath of God upon their imperial oppressors, had failed. The Romans had even mocked the hope of such a figure. That surely was it, the end of the story! How could this failed one be the Messiah?

The followers of Jesus clearly felt his failure deeply. They had committed their lives, giving up trades and professions for perhaps as long as three years, living in hand to mouth poverty, to follow this one and now it was all over without even a struggle. Rome, along with the local collaborating leadership, had again showed how effortlessly simple it was to deal with an agitator.

In the face of that what was one to do? For some the lesson was clear; forget peaceful non-violent resistance. The only way to oppose Rome and its collaborators was 'by the sword.' That would be the response of the increasing numbers drawn to the Zealot movement, that type of resistance culminating in 66 CE, some 30 years after the time of Jesus, with armed rebellion against Rome. That rebellion lasted nearly seven years as Rome struggled to re-conquer the Jewish people, finally succeeding in taking Masada, where the last Jewish holdouts took the course of mass suicide rather than fall again into Roman captivity. That violent revolutionary spirit would again rise with the movement led by Simon bar Kockba, six decades later only to once again be even more ruthlessly crushed by Roman might.[5]

---

[5] It is possible, though very much debated, that perhaps Judas Iscariot (the name is said to etymologically link with sicarii, literally 'dagger bearer') had been planning this sort of

In short, it seems the close followers of Jesus, following his execution, were psychologically crushed and living in fear. It is likely they would have kept hidden while in Jerusalem we are told 'for fear of the Jews,' (John 20:19) probably in reality more so the Romans, thankful that there were plenty of pilgrims present for Pesach or Passover, that giving some cover, before fleeing Jerusalem as quickly as they could back to Galilee which, not being directly under Roman rule, may have provided some sort of sanctuary. That panic and denial is already present in the gospels, even before Jesus' death during the trial of Jesus, with the thrice denial of Peter. In his defense, at least he is there to make that denial. The others in panic and fear have seemingly fled for their lives, being already in hiding. Given the cruelty of Roman rule, and the price paid for crossing it, we should not be too hasty in judging Peter!

The additional chapter in John's Gospel has those who were fisher folk among them having returned to their profession, probably with the hope of things returning to some type of normality. This is the type of response one would expect. Some of them may have carried some bitterness toward Jesus, because it seemed he had made promises he clearly was unable to keep. Others no doubt, were numbed by the disappointment they felt, hopes they had held having been brutally stripped from them. Such was the depth of their certainty that the Jesus story had come to an end, any talk of resurrection was dismissed out of hand as 'idle chatter.'

Yet, something happens which transforms these understandably fearful followers of Jesus, from living at best in resignation, but perhaps in fear, anger and despair, into fearless proclaimers of this one who on all levels had, as we have seen, failed. What was this incredible transformative power? I wish to charge that it could only be something so powerful we call it resurrection.

If not then objectified physical proof of the resurrection, what was it then that changed these followers? In essence we cannot know, but something must have happened, in order to set these people on a mission which led to them establishing communities proclaiming this one, shamefully executed in apparent failure, as being one who was truly the longed for

---

response to Roman power with his disappointment in Jesus' refusal to take this path leading to his betrayal, maybe with the hope that faced with arrest and death, Jesus would call lead such a violent uprising reinforced by 'twelve legions of angels.' (Matt 26:53)

Messiah, despite all the 'un-messiah' like things which had happened to him, and the shame attending his execution. What changed those living in fear to become fearless proclaimers? What caused these people to engage in a debate concerning Jesus within the Jewish tradition of which they were part, which seemingly they could never win, the Hebrew Scriptures lying surely with their opponents in that debate? Ask any Jewish person to this day as to Jesus being the Messiah and the response will be, even if it is acknowledged that he was a good person, perhaps even a prophet, that he cannot be the Messiah for he did not fill the messianic signs. How could Jesus have been the Messiah bringing the messianic era, they would charge if, as we well know, violence, injustice and death continue? Specifically their response may include how the Scriptures speak of how 'cursed is he who hangs upon a tree.' (Deut 21: 23) It is clear, such a cursed one cannot be the one come to bring the reign of God. Hence Paul writing of the cross, describes it as being 'a stumbling block to the Jews.' (1 Cor 1:23) The early followers of Jesus had to argue on these grounds and they did so. Something absolutely profound must have provided their reason for doing so. That thing they clearly judged, to be resurrection. Without it any argument that Jesus was the Messiah would have made absolutely no sense. It would have been untenable. Thus we find the early followers of Jesus arguing his case using those few passages of the Hebrew Scriptures they could, so to show that the cross was actually within the divine plan. Thus they have Jesus call out the words, 'My God, why have you forsaken me' from the cross, (Ps 22:1, cf Mark 15:34, Matthew 27:46) this cry being gradually turned from a cry of dereliction to one which confirming the crucifixion as part of the divine plan, while in the Book of Acts, Luke asserts likewise, that the cross was part of the divine plan. (Acts 2:23) Often we find a divine necessity linked to the cross, the evangelists having Jesus say of his crucifixion, 'was it not necessary' or 'the son of man must suffer.' (Luke 24:26, Mark 8:31 and pars, 9:12, 9:31, 10:33) As seen in our examination of John's Gospel, that evangelist particularly asserts numerous times that this is the case. In this gospel we have thus surmised at Jesus' crucifixion, 'For these things took place that the Scripture might be fulfilled.' (John 19:36-37)

The story of Jesus could not just end in martyrdom, for a failed reign of God would not have caused the early followers of Jesus to become fearless advocates for his cause. To the contrary though, Frances Young in a particularly interesting discussion of tragedy in theater speaks of sacrifice as being cathartic. Tragedy reveals deep truths about human nature, not doing away with it, but moving it through to a resolution. Jesus is a heroic figure whose going to the cross is redemptive in itself, his death upon the cross something turning the taboo into a thing holy. There is, he argues, no need for the resurrection as vindication. Indeed, he notes it takes away the profundity of the tragedy of the crucifixion, even trivializing it by a simplistic resolution, the 'they all lived happily ever after' type of thing. As attractive as I find his argument I still don't see how such could have wrought such dramatic change in the followers of Jesus. They needed to see Jesus as indeed the Messiah, not just as a heroic figure, however profound. So shaped were they by their Jewish understanding, it is unlikely they would have seen anything heroic about the cross, but rather given their background, would have viewed it as shameful. Their whole argument with their fellow Jews hinged on this Jesus being Messiah, and given his failure to bring the messianic era, it seems to me that something more is required than heroic martyrdom for his followers to have argued in the manner that they did, for him being the Messiah. What caused them to move from fear and trepidation, having just having witnessed the ruthless manner with which Rome and its collaborators had dealt with their leader, to become those who courageously proclaimed this 'failed figure' at great risk to themselves? That dramatic change only makes sense, I believe, in light of what comes as an absolute reversal to the shameful events which had occurred to that stage, what we may call resurrection, however we understand it.

Even the opponents of the Jesus movement would have realized this and thus sought to exclude the idea of resurrection. This is behind the story, almost certainly concocted by Matthew, of guards being placed at the tomb. (Matt 27: 62-66) As we have seen the followers of Jesus countered that they had fallen asleep. Of course, in reality there were no guards, fallen asleep or otherwise at the tomb of Jesus. What the guards show is that both the proponents and opponents of Jesus' resurrection understood, is that so much hung on this issue. That he rose or did not rise was at the heart of the early debate, and that it was, shows its centrality in the primitive Christian story.

Chapter Six: The deeper evidence

Indeed, the message that Jesus has risen was at the very heart of all the apostolic preaching from the very first sermon recorded in the Book of Acts. (Acts 2: 14-39) There, we find Peter proclaiming that the cross was necessary precisely to make the resurrection possible: 'this Jesus, lifted up according to the definite plan and foreknowledge of God, was crucified and killed by the hands of the lawless. But God raised him up having loosed the pangs of death, because it was not possible for him to be held by it.' (Acts 2:23-24) The Hebrew Scriptures are then called into play as offering evidence for the resurrection. Speaking of God setting this one on the throne of David, Peter claims, 'David foresaw and spoke of the resurrection of the Christ, that he was not abandoned to Hades, nor did his flesh see corruption. This Jesus God raised up, and of that we are all witnesses.' (Acts 2:31-32) Let us place aside that we may wish to argue concerning the means of Peter's ahistorical use of the Hebrew Scriptures, (Psalm 16:8-11) in the manner he does so here. For us of clearly such type of use has no legitimacy, but what is crucial here is that the message of the resurrection, including the finding of it within the Hebrew Scriptures, lay at the very heart of the earliest apostolic witness. That it is so hard for the followers of Jesus to find such passages, and the need therefore, to clearly stretch the evidence when they do so, shows just how crucially important the resurrection was in their debate with their fellow non-believing Jews. It is clearly the argument for resurrection which is the means of refuting the charge made by the Jewish opponents that his means of dying precluded Jesus from being the Messiah. That refutation we see plainly in the last words of Peter's sermon following his discourse on the resurrection, 'Let all the house of Israel therefore know assuredly that God has made him both Lord and Christ, this Jesus whom you crucified.' (Acts 2:36)

The resurrection also serves as vindication for Jesus' way. In the apostolic preaching we again hear the words, 'God anointed Jesus of Nazareth with the Holy Spirit and with power; how he went about doing good and healing all who were oppressed by the devil, for God was with him. And we are witnesses to all that he did both in the country of the Jews and in Jerusalem. They put him to death by hanging him on a tree; but God raised him up on the third day and made him manifest; not to all the people but to us who were chosen by God as witnesses, who ate and drank with him after he rose from the dead. And he commanded us to preach to the people and testify that he is the one ordained by God to be judge of the living and the dead.' (Acts 10:38-42) There could be hardly any clearer explanation of the purpose of the resurrection. It is the vindication of the righteous one, who is not left in the shame of the cursed death on a tree, (a shame not hidden but quite openly noted here) but rather is resurrected in order to judge all. The path that Jesus has courageously trod through his life, his standing with the marginalized and rejected against the powerful, shaped by his understanding of what he called, 'the kingdom of God', had finally led him to the cross. For the early Christians resurrection as vindication of this way of Christ lay at the core of their preaching.

The resurrection belief was also at the core of how the early apostles understood their role, that being not to govern, but rather to bear witness to the resurrection. (Acts 4:33) Belief in the resurrection was also the determining factor in electing the successor of Judas Iscariot as an apostle. (Acts 1:22)

Turning to the family of Jesus, we are left with the same quandary as to why their understanding concerning Jesus underwent such a dramatic change. What changed the family from being so seemingly non-comprehending of the ministry of Jesus, they surmised him to be beside himself, (Mark 3:20-21) to having such belief in him, despite his failure to carry through his promise? Again, we can only surmise that something must have happened, not from within Jesus' life itself, but following it to have turned these non-comprehending skeptics into followers of their failed Messiah child and brother. Probably all the brothers came to hold high positions in the Jerusalem Church, with James becoming the leader of that church. James and Paul spent much time in opposition to each other as regards their understanding of this new movement, particularly regards the place of the Torah or Law, but they do share a thing in common, something associated with Jesus which turns their world 180 degrees. Let us turn then to Paul.

Certainly Paul had a very strong experience of Jesus' resurrection and subsequent revelation to him, that revelation, initially on the road to Damascus, being so powerful it caused Paul to believe himself to be an apostle, having as strong a justification to call himself such, as those who had actually walked the roads of Galilee before journeying to Jerusalem with Jesus.

For Paul, a 'Hebrew of the Hebrews,' (Phil 3:4-5) with a mindset so shaped by the Jewish Messianic hope, there can be nothing in Jesus' actual ministry, which in light of that traditional hope, had proved disappointing, which would lead him to so elevate Jesus as he does, save that something dramatic must have happened following Jesus' shameful death turning everything on its head. It is for this reason that for Paul, the resurrection is absolutely central, and without it the whole Christian story collapses. (1 Cor 15:14) Yet, clearly Jesus, even in his resurrection, still does not succeed in carrying out the classical Jewish messianic role, that of bringing the messianic era. Paul must therefore reorient his significance and he does so radically precisely by the use of the cross and resurrection. This resurrection experience acts as the cause and stimulus for that radical re-orientation of Christian faith, led by Paul, from something centering on belief in the Messiah who comes to bring the 'Kingdom of God,' something thoroughly Jewish, to a new faith, where Jesus becomes the dying and rising God, so common in the pagan world, through whom eternal life is won. Indeed, I contend that this radical transformation of Christian faith would be impossible without the idea of resurrection.

Paul, as we have seen, essentially had no concern for the ministry and teaching of Jesus, indeed not even in the life of Jesus. Thus, when Paul argues his ethics and teaching, as he often does, he hardly ever makes reference to what the actual Jesus said in order to support his case, with the only time the earthly Jesus is referred to being in Paul's discussion of the Eucharist or Last Supper. (1 Cor 11:23-34) What is crucial to Paul is that God in Jesus dies and rises again, with that death and resurrection winning for a believer, and Paul radically opens up the category of believers to those beyond Judaism, access to another domain in which they, resurrected in Jesus, spend a transformed eternal existence with him. It is for this reason the resurrected Christ became everything for Paul. Resurrection is what enables Jesus to be turned into a cosmic dying and rising savior, who is the means by which eternity with God, set in another domain, may be won. By such Jesus has been changed from a Jewish Messiah into something much more in common with the savior gods of the wider Graeco-Roman world. So successful was Paul in achieving this, that this becomes the Jesus which most people, be they Christian or not, are most familiar.

Paul is joined by John with something similar. In the Gospel of John it is through the lens of Christ resurrected by which the whole gospel must be viewed. As with Paul in John, Jesus likewise no longer speaks of the reign of God as the core of his message, that again being replaced by eternal life. With John the Christian message, given the later date of composition, is beginning to move increasingly into a Hellenized world. Thus Jesus becomes a type of cultic savior figure, through whom one is able to escape the veil of this existence into eternal life. Eternal life is a mark of a person's relationship with God, established through Jesus. That eternal life is not entirely other worldly, as it begins in the current moment, John's Gospel after-all having the realized eschatology of which I have spoken. The fullness of God's presence, primarily future in the synoptic gospels as the cosmic reforming 'reign of God,' is in John's Gospel made present in the believer in the given moment of their reception of eternal life. That eternal life is not a consequence of a person's relationship with Jesus, but rather acts as the sign of that existing relationship, being its very essence. 'This is eternal life that they know you, the only true God, and Jesus Christ, whom you have sent.' (John: 5:24-26) This is a style of incorporation into the divine, giving the participant eternal life was very common in the ancient world, the numerous mystery cults having precisely that as their purpose.

Once again, given Jesus' failure in classical Jewish messianic expectation, something else must have happened causing John to want to turn this failed Jewish Messiah into a universal cultic figure, though which eternal life with the Divine is procured. John has no doubts as to this event – resurrection. As said, it is through the lens of resurrection with which we must view the whole Jesus story as told by John.

We have found then the change in outlook concerning Jesus evidenced in 'the disciples', Jesus' own family, Paul, and John, indicates that something dramatic must have occurred to turn their doubt, disappointment, fear, perhaps even anger, into something the very opposite of these things. Further, the actions of the opponents of Jesus in trying to shut down the account of the resurrection, indicate that it must have had strong traction for a significant number of people.

Chapter Six: The deeper evidence

Clearly none of this is the sort of evidence that would, as I said, stand up in a court of law, for it is all circumstantial. What it does, however, is to give us some indication that something absolutely unexpected occurred which caused these people, bitterly disappointed following the death of the one in whom they held such hope, perhaps even angry for being deceived by him, to suddenly be transformed to testify, with increasing bravery and conviction concerning him, to the point that each of the apostles, according to later tradition, would give their lives for this 'failed Messiah.' In like manner something must have happened to turn the family of Jesus, who at best thought him deluded, to become prominent followers, with one even becoming the leader of the church in Jerusalem. Likewise some event must have occurred to turn Saul, so steeped in Jewish messianic expectation, and an erstwhile opponent of the Jesus movement, into Paul, its advocate.

Thus, all those of whom we have spoken, Jesus' closest followers, his family, John, and his erstwhile opponent Saul ascribed their dramatic change to what they call resurrection. Their experience was that the one executed, and therefore failed Messiah, was still intimately present with them. What may be described as a delusional wish fulfillment as regards his closest followers during his lifetime, though psychologically that seems to represent an unusual response, certainly cannot apply to those figures like his family or Paul, who had nothing riding on such a wish fulfillment, having either misunderstood, or even opposed, Jesus and the movement which followed him.

The Scottish theologian Richard Holloway compares our trying to get at the factual event of resurrection to an astrophysicist trying to find the genesis of the universe in the 'Big Bang.' Clearly the astrophysicist can never actually see that event. What the astrophysicist does is project back, using primarily the red shift of galaxies and stars, showing how fast they are moving away from us. From that re-winding the expansion of the universe to the beginning, they can now 'see' back 13.4 billion light years to the beginning. In like manner, as the Big Bang being not available to our immediate experience, nor so is the resurrection of Jesus. In searching for the resurrected one, as in the case of the astrophysicist, we can only work back from the evidence we have. That evidence is the remarkable change wrought in those who knew, followed, or had opposed Jesus in his earthly life. The magnitude of that change, especially upon those who had no 'interest' in changing, allows us to begin to work backwards from that to the actual event.[6] This first level evidence concerning the resurrection of Jesus is far stronger, I hold, than that which is clearly created long, at least 50 years, after the event – the empty tomb, angelic appearances, grave-clothes left in a particular manner, and the type of objectified appearances which we find in our gospels. Those things designed as 'objective proofs' really represent less evidence for the resurrection than the existential change wrought in those who knew this failed Jewish Messiah.

It is still that existential change which continues to be the strongest evidence for the resurrection today. In saying that I am reminded of the story of the reformed alcoholic, who when confronted by a skeptic denying the resurrection, charging it had no objective proof, asked him how he could have such confidence in it as a real event, replied, 'all I know was that I once was an alcoholic and then I met the risen Lord and I was changed and am no longer drinking.' The skeptic no doubt walked away entirely dissatisfied, unconvinced with the answer, but in it lies a profound truth, for the only real evidence we have for the resurrection is actually experiential. The earliest evidence for the resurrection begins as such, the transformations of lives, with that evidence being supplemented to this day with each experiential change wrought by the resurrected power of the Galilean. This last sentence obviously will not provide any satisfaction for the skeptic but so be it.

John Newton once dealt in slaves taking them from freedom in Africa to the chains and whips of the Americas. One day, on experiencing the 'amazing grace' mediated by the resurrected one, he radically broke with that evil trade becoming one of the leading proponents of the emancipation movement. In such radical change, I charge, is the true and essentially only witness to the resurrection.

The way of Jesus was a path set on those things represented by what he called 'the kingdom of God' – justice, peace, reconciliation and the harmony of all things. In standing for this, Jesus was brutally executed by an empire having no truck in such. The resurrection was experienced by many in the early church as vindication for the way of Jesus, a bold declaration that the

---

[6] Richard Holloway, Doubts and Loves, Canongate, United Kingdom, 2005

power of the empire, with its hand on death, was not the final word. By such, the resurrection is radically rooted into the path chosen by Jesus in his living. I finally contend that this choice of living, this commitment to the way of Jesus, rather than any so called objective proof, is the method by which we perceive the truth of the resurrection. It is when we choose to live to the values exemplified by Jesus, rather than in seeking some type of proof for it, that we best find evidence for the resurrection. It is through orthopraxis then, right practice in the manner of Jesus, that we both, experience resurrection for ourselves, and understand his resurrection, rather than by some attempt at dispassionate, objective search for evidence of it, either from within, or outside the Scriptures. We live to the resurrection rather than understand the resurrection.

On the Third Day

Postlude

I have already just touched on the significance of the resurrection, speaking of how we come to know it in our active living, rather than in our dispassionate seeking of empirical proof. I want to now conclude briefly, by touching upon a few areas upon which the nature of resurrection can cast light.

We have examined why the physicality of the resurrection was important for the early church, primarily as a means of defense against an all-pervasive Gnosticism threatening to subsume the message of Jesus Christ. Gnosticism is certainly not absent from the contemporary church wherein we find still, either a fear or distain of the body, particularly sexuality, or a lack of concern for the material in general, in favor of the 'spiritual.' Further, we often find an aversion to politics, understood most broadly to include economics and all aspects of human living, together in relationship to the wider eco-sphere, with it viewed as mundane or even profane, in favor of a more pure spirituality. It is to these concerns, that the physicality of the resurrection speaks.

Indeed, without affirming the importance of those material things, my belief is that the physical nature of the resurrection makes no real sense. Of course, it may be argued that in order for the Christian gospel to give support for such things, an embodied resurrection is not really needed. One would think that the doctrines of creation and incarnation would suffice. Still the bodily resurrection serves to further add to the case for the importance of such material things.

I wish to conclude then, by examining why I believe the physicality of the resurrection is important for us, in whatever manner we understand that physicality. In speaking of physical resurrection, I am speaking not only of Christ's, but also that of believers. Of the believer's resurrection it should be noted, that is not in order to be absorbed into the Godhead, but rather to an individual embodied existence, distinct from the Divine, such post-resurrection embodiment serving as further affirmation of our embodied existence. The Scriptures clearly speak, as we have seen, of an individual existence, distinct from the Divine, in the resurrected state. One is not, as in a number of Eastern religious forms, dissolved finally into the Godhead, but continues with individual identity, which necessarily assumes some type of embodiment in that sphere, the understanding of that beyond us, as indeed it was for Paul.

In order to stress the importance of the physicality of resurrection I wish to commence with the whole issue of body. This is something which has besmirched Christianity given its development of such a strong anti-body bias. Indeed, on occasions this has been extreme. The en-fleshed body has often been viewed in essence evil, something from which one must escape by means of an anti-material spirituality. This has led to a radical dualism within Christianity, with a denigration of the body and all that it represents. This of course is most evident in Christian attitudes to sex and sensuality, with all the problems which this has caused. Those problems range from widespread guilt and anti-women bias, to pornography, and even paedophilia. Of the first of these things we will be well aware, and I hardly need to examine it as the evidence is so abundant. The repression of a healthy sexuality, given the power of this force, has not succeeded of course in extinguishing the force, but rather has only re-directed that powerful impulse, which has then manifested itself in unhealthy forms, especially views held of women as temptress, and also the ever increasing plethora of pornography, including that worst form of that pornographic use of sex, paedophilia, so strongly associated with the church. It is not only a Freudian analyst who would expect such. Repressed impulses, especially those so strong, are clearly going to manifest themselves in some usually unhealthy destructive manner, and it is highly likely that a healthy appreciation of body would preclude many of these issues. One would think that Christianity would have sufficient means to defend itself from such anti-material, flesh denying views given its doctrine of creation, of which God beheld 'it was good,' and through its doctrine of the incarnation, the taking of flesh form by the divine in Jesus Christ. The added understanding of the physicality of the resurrection, given that it lies often at the core of the justification of such anti-body views, will serve as corrective to those views which have so impacted Christianity, and lead to a greater appreciation of our embodied form.[1] A truly embodied

---

[1] Maurise Wiles to the contrary charges, the resurrection makes Christ docetic in that he doesn't share with us the fullness of human existence, for that existence includes death and dissolution of the body. Maurice Wiles 'A naked pillar of rock' in Resurrection, Essays

Christianity would understand the body, including sex and sensuality, as a natural part of living, indeed something intended by God as part of the created order, either in the temporal or resurrected state. That last state would cease being held as a thing calling us away from our embodied existence, and judging it as evil. Sensuality would be something to be celebrated rather than repressed, with women understood as an essential part of that celebration. Women, rather than being projected as evil temptresses or sirens, calling men to fall from some supposedly higher more spiritual way, would instead be viewed as partners and equals, sharing in being part of the good creation of God. Their sexuality, rather than something to be feared or fled from, would be embraced and celebrated.

Repressed sexuality is also re-directed into pornography and even paedophilia. Pornography, especially with its accessibility in the digital age, has reached plague proportions. It has mainly found expression in the 'Christian West,' from where it has infected many cultures, either indirectly culturally, or directly through such things as sex tourism. Such represents the dark side of that which is repressed for, as just seen, such a powerful force as sexuality, when repressed doesn't simply disappear, but rather finds itself re-directed into perverted and destructive forms. Probably the worst expression of pornography is paedophilia, which in recent years has been shown to have been long virulent within the church. Simply put, when it comes to sex, repression doesn't lead to the impulse disappearing, but rather leads to expression in dark and sometimes extremely perverted forms.

In all this it is important to differentiate between what I understand as flesh and fleshliness, world and worldliness. Many Christians confuse these, understanding the Scriptural denigration of 'flesh,' (Rom 8: 6-9, 12-13, 9:3-8, 13:14, I Cor 3:1- 3, Gal 5:16-19 et al.) and likewise 'worldly,' (Rom 12:2, 1 Cor 1:27-28, 2:12, 3:19, 4:9, 4:13 et al.) both found almost exclusively in the Pauline corpus, as meaning that Christianity has a negative view toward the flesh and the world in essence. This however, is not the case, for the Pauline critique of these things I hold to be a thing which judges these things precisely because they represent mal-expressions of things which are essentially good, seen that way both in Paul and elsewhere. (1 Cor 6:16, 2 Cor

---

in honour of Leslie Houlden, eds Stephen Barton and Graham Stanton. Society for the Propagation of Christian Knowledge, London, 1994: 116-127.

4:11, Gal 2:20) I believe that we do best to understand 'worldliness' as a sin, due to it being a perversion of that essentially good, the world, while equally 'fleshliness' is a sin, being a perversion of that again which is in essence good, the flesh.

The physicality of the resurrection affirms then what is elsewhere affirmed in the Christian doctrines of creation and incarnation, the world and flesh being in essence good. Such affirmation can lead Christians to live in a far healthier manner toward their bodies, in particular their sexuality, for both historically and currently it would be fair to say, Christians on the whole have been so fixated on a hatred of the flesh, they could be said to have a collective neurosis concerning it.

There are also wider issues to do with this embodiment of Christian belief. The radical disembodiment within Christianity affects our whole understanding of the material world, understood as having a diminished importance. This manifests itself most obviously in our concern, or lack thereof, in the social, economic, political, and ecological issues, of our world. A concern for embodied existence would clearly lead to a concern for these things, whereas a lack of concern for the embodied, sees them as unimportant in light of more other-worldly spiritual issues. This is linked to the misunderstanding, just referred to, which we have concerning world and worldliness. This misunderstanding and depreciation of the material has a particular effect when it comes to justice issues. Why should one have a concern for justice issues, when the importance of such materialities is diminished precisely because of they being material rather than spiritual?

Embodied resurrection affirms these material concerns, calling us away from some other-worldly spiritualism, to a concern for the embodied existence of our neighbors. When we understand the importance of the body affirmed in the biblical story of creation, incarnation, and resurrection, we are far more likely to protest against those things so prevalent in our world where the body is misused – in slavery (there are more slaves in our world than ever), in styles of labor, which wear down those forced into it, usually grossly underpaid, the ever increasing use, as documented by Amnesty International, of torture, or of an unjust economic and foreign policy, which results in such things as widespread famine, malnourishment, violence, war and refugee flight. Issues such as the privatization of water and seed varieties, two things essentially linked to the core needs of the body, both of ourselves and others, are more easily seen for what they should be, issues at the heart of our faith. Tellingly, Andrew Harvey charges, the church does not speak much about life after death these days, due to some, mainly in the 'Christian West' in their opulence, having heaven already existing on earth, while for the majority, due to crushing injustice, hell is likewise already present.[2]

Clearly the material doesn't just extend to the human domain, but to the whole material realm, the ecosphere. In a world suffering from rapidly increasing strain ecologically, it is more imperative than ever to not succumb to an other-worldly spiritualism as represented by a disembodied resurrection. An en-fleshed resurrection is far more likely to cause us to have concern for current ecological crises of species extinction, loss of habitat and most threatening of all, rapid climate change.

To conclude, broadly within Christianity there are two views of salvation. We have become intimately familiar with the first, where redemption or salvation is separated from creation, in that one is saved out of creation to another other-worldly domain. This manifests itself for the individual as something where salvation is associated with a post-death experience in another place beyond this 'earthly vale,' understood to be merely a place of preparation for real life in the other. Creation as a whole is understood to be coming to some type of cataclysmic end, from which something infinitely better will emerge. This created order is not valued, but rather is understood to represent something 'fallen.' Within such a theological framework there clearly is little concern for the things of this earth, for salvation belongs not there, but elsewhere, not now, but future. At its extreme, this view holds such a deprecatory view of the earth it looks forward to its extinction as being necessary for the better to come. Such movements as nuclear or ecological apocalypticism are extreme, but logical, outcomes from such a theology.

The alternate view sees these two things, creation and redemption/salvation, as belonging together, with creation as a whole moving toward

---

[2] Andrew Harvey, 'They discussed among themselves what this "rising from the dead" could mean' in Resurrection, Essays in honour of Leslie Houlden, eds Stephen Barton and Graham Stanton. Society for the Propagation of Christian Knowledge, London, 1994: 69-78.

a time of perfection. The Scriptures are understood as being book-ended by descriptions of a perfected created order. (Gen 1-2, Rev 21-22) In such understanding the material, creation itself, is understood to be of crucial importance. Salvation, rather than being understood to somewhere else over and beyond the earth and the material, is rather about the perfection of those things. Though it includes the individual, it is much more corporate in its emphasis, in that the individual is rooted into the wholeness not only of the human family, but also into the wider ecosphere. Clearly, an en-fleshed resurrection, back into this material realm speaks more to these concerns.

To be fair the Scriptural tradition can support either of the above views but my understanding is that in our context the second makes much better sense, representing a far better and propitious hope. It is that theology which speaks coherently to us, being so needed in our context. Further, the second serves as a corrective to the first, which all too often has had a near universal voice within Christianity.

A physical resurrection is important then for these theological purposes. As we have seen, it cannot be taken literally, and in a modern age it is entirely nonsensical to take it in such manner, requiring corporeal bodies passing through still wrapped grave-clothes, through walls where people are hiding in fear, and ascending to heaven in a three story universe. Historically, the physicality of the resurrection grew ever stronger as the church defended the gospel from an all-pervasive Gnosticism, with its radical depreciation of the physical and material. Literal interpretations concerning the physicality of the resurrection, reach points in the gospels where to us it sounds implausible, and that literalism would develop to what we would regard as ridiculous lengths in the second century. Though we should reject the literalism which became associated with the physical resurrection, we should be thankful that the Scriptures and early church took a stance rejecting the allure of Gnostic systems, instead choosing to affirm the importance of the physical and material. We, in light of those things of which I have just raised, ought to be likewise zealous in defending the physicality and material understanding laying at the heart of Christian faith.

We clearly are best advised to take the physical resurrection as a theological, rather than an empirical historical reality. As such it need not draw us into defending that which seems not only crude but also unsustainable in a modern age. Understood theologically, however, it affirms the crucial importance of the material, our human being in such things as how we regard our embodied sexuality, including our treatment of women, in our concern to ensure justice and peace become realities in our material existence, but also in how we regard the whole of creation, the eco-sphere in general. The resurrection affirms hope in our world, that the power of death, wielded by the empire is not the final word. Its physicality calls us away from an other-worldly spiritualism to radically engage with the material. We are challenged to live in the transformative power of the resurrection, understanding it in the only way in which it is accessible to us, by committing ourselves to the same values, as the one to whom it came as vindication. Those values call us to the material physical world which it so strongly affirms.

www.ingramcontent.com/pod-product-compliance
Lightning Source LLC
Chambersburg PA
CBHW072156160426
43197CB00012B/2409